Under a Gull's Wing

Poems *and* Photographs
of the Jersey Shore

Edited by
Rich Youmans
and
Frank Finale

Down The Shore Publishing
Harvey Cedars, NJ

A CORMORANT BOOK

DOWN THE SHORE PUBLISHING

For information, address:
Down The Shore Publishing, Box 3100, Harvey Cedars, NJ 08008.
The words "Down The Shore" and the Down The Shore Publishing logo are registered U.S. Trademarks.
Printed in Canada. First printing, 1996.
10 9 8 7 6 5 4 3 2 1

Cover photograph © Ray Fisk.
Cover design by Leslee Ganss.

Library of Congress Cataloging-in-Publication Data

    Under a gull's wing : poems & photographs of the Jersey shore / edited
      by Rich Youmans and Frank Finale.
          p.   cm.
      "A Cormorant book."
      ISBN 0-945582-36-6
      1. American poetry--New Jersey.   2. Coasts--New Jersey--Poetry.
    3. Coasts--New Jersey--Pictorial works. I. Youmans, Richard, 1960-
  . II. Finale, Frank, 1942- .
    PS548.N5U53   1996
    811'.5408032749--dc20   96-21310
                                                CIP

To my wife, Ann, for her love and understanding through the course of this project and always

— Rich

To my wife, Barbara, who provided me with the needed nurturing, encouragement, and time

— Frank

Contents

From the Editors

We would like to say the idea for this anthology came one day while walking along a deserted beach, as whitecaps arced and seagulls swooped and sunlight dazzled the sea — an elemental moment that only poetry could capture. Instead, it came one stormy winter's night while we were having dinner at a small Italian restaurant in Long Branch, as the wind cut through empty streets and a cold rain turned to snow. As was typical between us, the table talk eventually turned to poetry — on that night, poetry about the Jersey shore. We recalled some of the more famous examples — A. R. Ammons's "Corsons Inlet," John Ciardi's "Two Egrets," Walt Whitman's "Patroling Barnegat." We recited remembered lines, and as we did a wondrous thing happened: the snow and rain disappeared, and we were transported into the worlds of those poems. Discussing Ammons, we found ourselves among "dunes of motion, organizations of grass, white sandy paths of remembrance." Guided by Ciardi, we witnessed two egrets fly over the Shrewsbury River "like two white hands washing one another in the prime of light." We stood with Whitman on the stormy shores of Barnegat, in the midst of "waves, air, midnight, their savagest trinity lashing."

So it went. We accompanied Maxine Kumin in her recollections of Depression-era Atlantic City, Stephen Dunn in his reveries while walking through the marshland of Brigantine Refuge (now the Edwin B. Forsythe National Wildlife Refuge), Joel Lewis in his reflections among the gaslight and gingerbread of Cape May. More than any other form of writing, poetry has that ability to lift and relocate a reader — to distill the essence of a place and present it as if for the first time. After journeying up and down the Jersey shore without leaving our chairs, we decided to assemble an anthology that would allow others to enjoy a similiar experience.

For our purposes, we've defined the shore as that 127-mile coastal strip from Sandy Hook to Cape May that most people typically associate with such "surf, sun, 'n' fun" pursuits as fishing, walking the boardwalks, dancing all night in clubs, or just lying on the beach under a blinding yellow sun. These aspects are well represented in the following pages. Yet, as with any region this large, the Jersey shore has more to offer. We wanted to present the shore's natural beauty — the immensity of the sea, the slow roll of dunes, the acres of dense marshland — as well as the overdevelopment and other human intrusions that threaten it. We sought to recount legends of pirates and ghosts; to recall traditional shore industries such as boatbuilding; and to recognize the various historic sites and structures found along the shore, such as Fort Hancock on Sandy Hook, Lucy the Margate Elephant, and the lighthouses that once guided tall-masted ships.

We also wanted to note as many communities as possible, to show the range of life and living "down the shore" — from the family-style fun of Point Pleasant Beach and Ocean City to the manic energy of Seaside Heights and Wildwood (famous for their clubs, cruising, and other teenage lures); from the Victorian elegance of Spring Lake and Cape May to the urban blight of Asbury Park and Atlantic City. In some areas, the poems combine to give historical insights. Those about Atlantic City, for example, describe the city as a cheap haven for Depression pensioners, a seaside carnival epitomized by the long-gone Steel Pier — site of such bizarre attractions as the High-Diving Horse and the man who buried himself alive — and a gambling mecca in which glitz and glamour cannot overcome the decay of surrounding neighborhoods. There are even poems about Absecon Island back when it was mostly swampland and dunes, its main structure a lighthouse that warned of treacherous shoals.

With this in mind, we have arranged the poems geographically, approximating a trip straight down the coastline. From Sandy Hook, the poems proceed through the more heavily developed northern shore areas, along the barrier islands and coastal pinelands, down into the southern shore communities (where towns and cities are often judged by the sizes of their boardwalks). They culminate in Cape May and Cape May Point, an area known as much for its avian displays as for its Victorian charms. The tour guides are a diverse lot, ranging from such well-known figures as Ammons, Ciardi, and Whitman to those poets who are still early in their careers but whose work promises to earn them much future acclaim. The guides also include some of the state's best photographers, who have provided more than two dozen photos of quintissential shore sites.

Yet, like any journey, this one is not definitive. Some readers will undoubtedly remember sites, events, or stories not reflected among these poems; if so, we hope this book will be a catalyst for those memories and many more. For those who have yet to visit the Jersey shore, we hope these poems will provide an introduction as well as an enticement to learn more. Above all, we hope this anthology— with its equal parts celebration, lament, and history — will serve as a tribute to a region that, through the years, has managed to rise above its problems and endear itself to generations of residents and vacationers alike. In the end, no place could ask for a better legacy.

— Rich Youmans and Frank Finale

Under a Gull's Wing

Poems *and* Photographs
of the Jersey Shore

The Gull

Madeline Tiger

the huge grey gull
over the Jersey Turnpike
steely as Amtrak

crosses long above this
congestion, soars
toward the seashore

his wings waving slowly

his beak points beyond
our dull metal,
grey as we've made him

he's traversing our lines
of bright cars, hot motors
rushed and stalled
        in their own fumes

far up he glides, he is
pointing to shining water,

to the waves that glisten —
ripples, breakers
with fierce bursting crests —

and when he squawks out there,

his cry leaves a whiteness
in the mind of the driver

sandy hook

Jane B. Rawlings

gull wing curve of beach terns
in flocks like sheep standing one-legged
weather vanes into the wind swirls
and eddies of clam shells mussels
chaff of dune grass pebbles drifting
the gentle swells of sand white caps
bottle caps fishing skiffs sand castles
afternoon lineup of jets overhead in the wind
a plastic bag rolls over and over

Sand Castle: Sandy Hook

Jane B. Rawlings

The child was thrilled to start — helped
dig the sand and pack the bucket,
patting the top down fiercely,
scraping the level flat as he could

while the man began to perfect
its circuit: smooth-packed walls
and balanced towers
with two clam shells each for windows,

pebbled court. He is caught by all
the child cannot conceive of: horses,
men in armor, pennants for the lists,
a call of trumpets. . . . Now

the child is tumbling near the moat;
he practices karate kicks, revolves
in feints; he rolls and scuffs the sand,
tide edging ever closer. . . .

Fort Hancock, Officers' Row. Photograph © Joseph Paduano.

At Fort Hancock, Sandy Hook

Rich Youmans

For my wife, Ann

We idly walk along small-town streets,
over sidewalks broken by sycamore,
past uniform buildings of pale ochre brick
and trim the color of holly. Sky
of few clouds, sun all around: a perfect day.
The American flag snaps like a salute.
Beyond, rising over a shingled roof,
the octagonal walls and fire-red crown
of our oldest working lighthouse.
We snap off a photo, head toward the bay.

Here, on a shapeshifting spit of land,
a nation once prepared to defend its shores.
Through a century's turn and two world wars,
the U.S. Army overran this beach: jeeps
rolled and rattled through holly groves,
soldiers ran from barracks to batteries
while missiles fired in practice arcs
above egrets, plovers, and terns.
On the parade field, enlisted men stood
in neat rows, straight as the stripes on the flag.

Now rock doves echo through the batteries'
tunnels, and tourists have overtaken the fort.
We pose by decorative mortar and cannon,
take shots of the homes on officers' row,
where captains and lieutenants once sat on
wooden porches, under late night stars, by the bay.
We walk, and try to imagine it all —
the din, the crowds, commands like artillery —
as, above us, a herring gull arcs out of view:
a burst of cloud, and then pale sky. . . .

Two Egrets

John Ciardi

On Easter morning two egrets
flew up the Shrewsbury River
between Highlands and Sea Bright

like two white hands
washing one another
in the prime of light.

Oh lemons and bells of light,
rails, rays, waterfalls, ices —
as high as the eye dizzies

into the whirled confetti
and rhinestones of the breaking blue
grain of lit heaven,

the white stroke of the egrets
turned the air — a prayer
and the idea of prayer.

Old Woman's Hill

H. A. Maxson

Along the Navesink

It's on no map, maybe only on
my father's mind if anyone cares
to know, like Waterwitch,
Plattmount and Gravelly Point,
places no one else remembers
the names or boundaries of anymore.

People live now on the foot-gulleyed
Lenape trail, and don't know it.
Over their camp a lawn needs cutting,
arrowheads are rising in their cycles
of sink and purge until the thick
weave of grass roots shunt them down.

Or maybe a point juts up to nick a heel,
or chippings needle below the cutting
blade.
   Down High View Circle
or The Drive spirits meander back
with their bags of clams and oysters
from the bay, not noticing the pale blue
walls, the Pontiacs and pup tents
they pass through in the yards,
but thinking and talking of the steep
hump of a hill, or the old landmark oak
setting this year's acorns against winter.

Sunday Drive to Sandy Hook

Judi K. Beach

Rt. 36 *through Monmouth Beach and Sea Bright*

They're building on the beaches,
biting away the sandbar
with asphalt and Florida pebbles,
with geraniums in redwood pots
where prickly pear had grown.

It all looks green to me
bile green shutters,
green shingled roofs,
stacked like dominoes
from ocean to river
waiting for a hurricane.

Worker ants invade the ocean,
carry jetty rocks from Maine
in crane baskets.
They're taking the beach to Pennsylvania
to trade for lumber and brick
and formica countertops.

If only condos were condoms,
so they wouldn't reproduce so quickly,
and I could glance at the ocean
or the river again
as I drive to Sandy Hook.

Twilight: Long Branch in Early October

Emanuel di Pasquale

A few seagulls,
three or four,
drag their shadows
along the ocean's edge,
an ocean so calm
the waters rise and fall
in thin-lipped hush.
The sun already set
is slow to draw all light
down the western curve,
and a mosaic,
black edged on green,
cracks the ocean's surface:
church windows,
a pewter chessboard.

Sand dune, Long Branch. Photograph © Joseph Paduano.

First Trip to the Jersey Shore: Long Branch, NJ

Maria Mazziotti Gillan

Every year when the silk mills closed in July, and everyone we knew went to the Jersey shore, we stayed home. We didn't own a car and even I knew we were poor, but when I was 13, suddenly, my mother agreed to go to the shore for a week with my aunt and my grown cousins. My cousin Joey drove. I sat in the back seat and tried not to be sick. Fifteen minutes from home, Joey had to stop the car so I could throw up at the side of the road. The Parkway hadn't been built yet. It took hours to get to the huge, white Victorian boarding house, with its graceful, wrap-around porch, its turrets and peaked towers and widow's walk. We slept in one room, my aunt and her family in another. Between the rooms, a shared bath with a claw-footed tub. My mother left Italy when she was 23. Before that she never left Santo Mauro, the little town in Campagnia where she was born. When she married my father, he brought her to an Italian neighborhood in Paterson; she refused to leave it, felt safe only in her own house and was so terrified of the ocean that every time we went near the water, she screamed, "Watch out! You'll drown." Through the open windows of the boarding house, we could smell the salt of the sea, tangy and sweet. We shared one kitchen with all the other families. The silver was kept in glasses on the counter; the napkins in a circular holder. Most evenings we walked on the quiet, empty boardwalk at Long Branch and watched the sea. One night, Joey drove us to Seaside Heights to that teeming boardwalk with its neon lights and loud, jostling crowds. We were given a dollar apiece to spend on the games of chance or the Ferris wheel. We wandered into the souvenir shops to look; we didn't buy anything. I saw a cedar keepsake box stamped Long Branch, New Jersey. I wanted it, but I only asked one time. My mother said no. The night before we were to leave Long Branch, my mother pushed the cedar box into my hands, said, "Here. This is for you," and turned away. I loved that box, kept it for years. The smooth, sweet aroma of cedar wood rose to meet me each time I opened it, made me remember the shore and the tangy aroma of salt air and my mother who turned away when she gave me that cedar box, though not before I saw her smile.

At Pleasure Bay

Robert Pinsky

In the willows along the river at Pleasure Bay
A catbird singing, never the same phrase twice.
Here under the pines a little off the road
In 1927 the Chief of Police
And Mrs. W. killed themselves together,
Sitting in a roadster. Ancient unshaken pilings
And underwater chunks of still-mortared brick
In shapes like bits of puzzle strew the bottom
Where the landing was for Price's Hotel and Theater.
And here's where boats blew two blasts for the keeper
To shunt the iron swing-bridge. He leaned on the gears
Like a skipper in the hut that housed the works
And the bridge moaned and turned on its middle pier
To let them through. In the middle of the summer
Two or three cars might wait for the iron trusswork
Winching aside, with maybe a child to notice
A name on the stern in black-and-gold on white,
Sandpiper, Patsy Ann, Do Not Disturb,
The Idler. If a boat was running whiskey,
The bridge clanged shut behind it as it passed
And opened up again for the Coast Guard cutter
Slowly as a sundial, and always jammed halfway.
The roadbed whole, but opened like a switch,
The river pulling and coursing between the piers.
Never the same phrase twice, the catbird filling
The humid August evening near the inlet
With borrowed music that he melds and changes.
Dragonflies and sandflies, frogs in the rushes, two bodies
Not moving in the open car among the pines,
A sliver of story. The tenor at Price's Hotel,
In clown costume, unfurls the sorrow gathered
In ruffles at his throat and cuffs, high quavers
That hold like splashes of light on the dark water,
The aria's closing phrases, changed and fading.
And after a gap of quiet, cheers and applause

Audible in the houses across the river,
Some in the audience weeping as if they had melted
Inside the music. Never the same. In Berlin
The daughter of an English lord, in love
With Adolf Hitler, whom she has met. She is taking
Possession of the apartment of a couple,
Elderly well-off Jews. They survive the war
to settle here in the Bay, the old lady
Teaches piano, but the whole world swivels
And gapes at their feet as the girl and a high-up Nazi
Examine the furniture, the glass, the pictures,
The elegant story that was theirs and now
Is a part of hers. A few months later the English
Enter the war and she shoots herself in a park,
An addled, upper-class girl, her life that passes
Into the lives of others or into a place.
The taking of lives — the Chief and Mrs. W.
took theirs to stay together, as local ghosts.
Last flurries of kisses, the revolver's barrel,
Shivers of a story that a child might hear
and half remember, voices in the rushes,
A singing in the willows. From across the river,
Faint quavers of music, the same phrase twice and again,
Ranging and building. Over the high new bridge
The flashing of traffic homeward from the racetrack,
With one boat chugging under the arches, outward
Unnoticed through Pleasure Bay to the open sea.
Here's where the people stood to watch the theater
Burn on the water. All that night the fireboats
Kept playing their spouts of water into the blaze.
In the morning, smoking pilasters and beams.
Black smell of char for weeks, the ruin already
Soaking back into the river. After you die
You hover near the ceiling above your body
And watch the mourners a while. A few days more

You float above the heads of the ones you knew
And watch them through a twilight. As it grows darker
You wander off and find your way to the river
And wade across. On the other side, night air,
Willows, the smell of the river, and a mass
Of sleeping bodies all along the bank,
A kind of singing from among the rushes
Calling you further forward in the dark.
You lie down and embrace one body, the limbs
Heavy with sleep reach eagerly up around you
And you make love until your soul brims up
And burns free out of you and shifts and spills
Down over into that other body, and you
Forget the life you had and begin again
On the same crossing — maybe as a child who passes
Through the same place. But never the same way twice.
Here in the daylight, the catbird in the willows,
The new café, with a terrace and a landing,
Frogs in the cattails where the swing-bridge was —
Here's where you might have slipped across the water
When you were only a presence, at Pleasure Bay.

It Was a Rising

Gerald Stern

It was a rising that brought the worms. They came
when the bodies came, the air was muddy, it was
a small mistake, the fingers were gone, the lips
were eaten away — though I love worms, they have
bags on their backs and pointed sticks, they come
by the thousands, they can clean a beach in an hour,
they can clean the ground of fruit and bottles,
paper and plastic. I was a worm once, I wore
an olive uniform, my specialty was Luckies,
I speared them by threes, I hooked a bone to a cup,
I caught the silver foil. The rain when it comes
forces the worms to the surface; that is another
rising but not as cataclysmic. Love
of one thing for another brought them up,
and love will bring them back. This is the flesh
that dies and this is the flesh that lives. The bone
at the base of the spine is called the almond, it is
the nucleus of our birth. I had my chance
when the worms were in the air. I went out swimming,
I started to float, I held my arms up sideways
and let myself be eaten. I lie on the beach
planning my future. I am a mile away
from the motors out there and I am a yard away
from the wet footprints. There is a bird half crying
and there are the waves half moaning, these are the sounds.
My nose alone is showing, most of my head
is buried, I should have a straw in my mouth
to breathe with and a periscope for my eye
to see the flags and see the derrick. I lie
in coldness, only my lips are burning; I crack
my blanket, I am free again, I rise
with sand on my shoulder, stomach, thighs. The calcium
ruins my arm; I try to wipe my back
and scream in pain; I crash into the water;
it is my justice there, in the blue, in the brown,

and I am happy. I find my stone with one breath
and rub the hatchings. It is a rolled-up scroll.
It is a book. I swim a few short lengths,
to Ireland and back, and end up walking the planks.
It is either the dream of Asbury Park
where it is built on clouds and there are cherubs
holding it end on end, or it is the city
itself, a state senator at one end,
a Confederate Legionnaire at the other,
in front of Perkins, with an unlined notebook,
ready for my own visionary window,
ready for a whole morning of sunlight and silence.

Asbury Park Casino. Photograph © Joseph Paduano.

Asbury Park— Into the Vision

Peter Lucia

circa 1950s

At first
a kind of whispering arena
mile-wide — whisper whispering rises
splinters into prattling crystallizes
joy — vacation voices — summery chattering.
Then — from one corner — *Daisy Daisy*
a tinny tiny spray of funny music — *I'm half crazy*
pops and pops — *love of you*
lots of them lots — *ding* — shrieks
the patter of strolling feet a thousand
on the boards beneath us.
The day is long and bigger than the sky.
White coconutty smell of beach creams and
like pink clouds promising celestial diversions
the scent of spun sugar.
Here now days of world at rest
with far far kingdoms etched in sky
beyond us. Yes.
Grand Pavilions skillgames wheels
carousels and souvenirs of sea
fish nets shells telescopes captains' bells
allow us glimpses past the thing at hand
transport us to the Grove
picture castles parks parades
different lands a block or two away.
A block or two away and then some.
What it is I can't yet say.
Still the wonder of it all appearing
boardwalk theaters boats arcades
is much the same as hearing
a certain smiling
music — something dear
reflecting life.

Something.
Here.
The time it takes
to portray.
Now among the decked-out crowds
the warmth of wood — ocean-wafted —
we — awe-enchanted — no longer to be weary
— venture forth and into a single day
strolling by castles bandstands little lakes
copper pavilions — take our place within
the pageantry of swans.

Sex Dream

Alicia Ostriker

Asbury Park, NJ

I see the bare feet on the warm boardwalk
Are my long-haired daughter's.
I dare not look above them, and I do not speak,

Thinking of silvered wood, white sand, cold surf.
The lacquered toenails curl, sand streaks
The downy legs, her cotton hemline droops.

And now the antique carousel revolves
Wildly to ghostly waltzes,
Its riders, men and women, surging and hawing.

About to leap onto it, she has flexed
Herself for that fatality: soon she will seize
A bar, she will climb onto a painted horse,

She who is unable to perceive,
Though she glances to the left and right, the mother
Who stands behind her whispering *jump, jump,*

Or the mother on the carousel, among
The multitude turning, laughing and shrieking, a woman
Who will bow, rise and salute her

When she makes her move.

On Hearing That the Asbury Park Carousel Has Been Sold to Private Collectors

Maria Mazziotti Gillan

In Asbury Park, I stand at the window
of the restored Berkeley Carteret Hotel,
with its spun sugar ceiling,
its carved border of pale pink
and lavendar flowers,
its mahogany four-poster beds,
its thick carpets and silence.
I spend luxurious hours
bathed in that silence,
after the clamour of my office,
telephones and voices,
police sirens screeching
outside my windows.

At dusk, I walk out of the hotel,
past flower-borders and neat grass;
across the road, the grimy boardwalk
appears to be rotting away. Discarded cups
and papers, blown by the wind,
rattle before they settle in corners
or sail down onto the sand. The carousel
sits neglected in its round, dilapidated building,
its windows so dirty I have to clean off a space
so I can look inside. Cobwebs, spun thick as cotton candy,
hang from the peeling paint of the ceiling, and drape
over the horses. I feel that I am watching them
through a screen that turns everything gray.

I remember riding on that carousel when the horses
were delicate and proud. We rode round and round
while the tinkling calliope music played
and the lights flashed red and gold.
The horses pranced up and down
on their silver poles.

Beyond the derelict carousel, I watch
the green expanse of the Atlantic,
the white sailboat, small and perfect as a toy,
that glides across the horizon.
The tide moves in, sweeping
across the sand, clearing it
of all that has been left there:
the crushed paper plates,
the broken sand shovel,
an old shoe — all disappear,
but the ocean surges,
blue and green,
as far as the eye can see.

Asbury Park

Ed Smith

Girls hug their boyfriends
with concert tickets in denim jackets.

They walk past black Atlantic,
breathing the seaweed, kelp.

Retired now, machinists kiss their
wives on the boardwalk, as the

loud music covers them. The
video arcades blast quarters

into unknown galaxies.
No one fantasizes here.

At the Asbury Park Hotel

Peter E. Murphy

Place yourself in January in this famished resort, high up
looking over the broken ocean and tumultuous boardwalk.
There is the restaurant battered by hunger, cloud tattered,
out of place, out of food. There are the streets where cats
whine in doorways, where echoes shoot out the blinking lights

of traffic that have nothing to stop for, nothing to lose.
And there, on the sand crummy beach a billion clams lie dying
from a freakish storm, as fat gulls stutter dizzily
among the decaying and the dead. There, waves beat their crowns
into gray foam. There, the horizon vanishes like a sigh,

like a limit no longer believed in, and here, on the high floors
of the magnificently lonely hotel, yours are the only eyes in the city.
Your blood is the only blood warmed by this vision, and you are grateful
to escape the company of swallows and sharks, all the loud creatures
that cannot stop, that cannot slow down without dying.

Ocean Grove
Rich Youmans

"To afford those who would spend a few days or weeks at the sea-shore an opportunity to do so . . . free from the temptations of dissipation. . . . To provide for the holding of camp-meetings of an elevated character, especially for the promotion of Christian holiness."
> — From the by-laws of Ocean Grove, NJ

1.

This morning I walk from the boardwalk down Ocean, past the shaded verandas and scrolled gingerbread, toward the Auditorium and its neon white cross. Behind me, the Atlantic swells and rolls, its horizon masked by early haze. But the neon cross rises, sure as a sign, high above the turrets and cupolas. Eighteen feet tall, it proclaims a single thought: This is a Christian town.

2.

They came here in 1869: Methodists seeking the tonic of sea. On three hundred acres, they pitched their tents, among tangles of briar and wild-wood, and within a few years had carved out a town, a way of life, a dream. Shoulder to shoulder, they sat on pine planks, crying *Hallelujah* in the voice of one, as sunlight fell along the ocean, in bits and pieces, like manna. Each Sunday, for more than a century, these streets turned silent as the sky: No swimming. No boating. No bicycling. No news permitted, except the Good News: it was the Day of Rest.

3.

The Sunday streets no longer close, yet still the modern pilgrims come. Each summer, along biblical alleypaths — Mt. Carmel, Mt. Zion, Bethany — the striped tents bloom against cottages, grow carnivelesque in the sun. Here at the heart of Ocean Grove — where the homeless, the derelict and mentally ill, wander from the Park like prophets gone mad — the pipe organ booms in the Auditorium as if to sound the Second Coming of Christ. Leaded panes glow with pentecostal fire, as preachers give *basso profundo* praise and lead the

assembled in prayer. At night, the notes of choirs and strings linger
like incense in the air, as high above the great cross burns, fierce as a
flaming sword.

4.

Among these timeless streets, I wander — for hours, days, maybe
years — until I return to Ocean and the surf: its lip of white foam, its
hosannas of spray. The haze has lifted, the sky is clear, and a white
sail, full of invisible wind, cuts across the sea and its vanishing point.
The surf spills and washes across the sand — over scalloped shells,
beach glass, the small tracks of gulls — then lapses, leaving in its
wake wetness and shine. Impelled, I discard my shoes, my socks, like
so many pilgrims to this shore, and step into the joyous wash of the
waves. Today, I am far from Route 35, from Asbury, Neptune, the coast
I have known; I am standing in waters that never dry, by a town settled
deep in its faith. The breakers crash and fall away, and the undertow
lures me like sin; yet I stand fast, here by Ocean Grove, the white
cross an anchor at my back.

Ocean Grove. Photograph © Joseph Paduano.

Learning to Float

Shirley Warren

for my grandson, Matthew,
at five years of age
in Ocean Grove, New Jersey

We'll begin in the shallows where
even the gentlest of breakers will be
enough to make your little fingers
cling to me like barnacles to a steady keel.

As I've done before, I'll kneel, level
with your eyes, and bear witness
to your fear of the ocean's roar
having nothing to do with drowning.

You'll stiffen, I'm sure, as obediently
you lift your feet to experience
the rise and the fall, the rocking wall
of freedom you're learning how to trust.

For now, though, you must believe that
I am stronger than the sea and that I will
never let you go anywhere darker
or deeper than these arms. Oh yes,

your Mama knows what I mean.
She also learned to float from me.

Gleanings

Scott Edward Anderson

Ocean Grove, NJ

Look at the two of them, bent
to the early morning tide.
They cull glass from the sandy surf.
Strange and wonderful alchemists,
who search for the elusive blue
of medicine bottles, caressing
emerald imitators from "Old Latrobe,"
or amber sea urchins
left there like whelks at low tide.

They discard broken bits of crockery,
forsaken like jetsam of the sands.
Beach glass is opaque
with a false clarity:
Polished by sand and sea,
the edges don't cut
like our lives, lived elsewhere,
out beyond the last sandbar,
where plate tectonics rule the waves.

(for Diane Stiglich & Jim Supplee)

Here I Am Walking

Gerald Stern

Here I am walking between Ocean and Neptune,
sinking my feet in mile after mile of wet life.
I am practically invisible
in the face of all this clutter,
either straying near the benches over the buried T-shirts
or downhill in the graveyard
where the burned families are sleeping in the sun
or eating dry lunch among the corpses.
I will finish walking in two hours
and eat my sandwich in the little park
beside the iron Methodist.
This is the first step.
Tomorrow I will start again in Barnegat
and make my way toward Holgate or Ventnor.
This is something different
than it was even five years ago.
I have a second past to rake over
and search through — another 2,000 miles of seashore
to account for.
— I am still making my mind up
between one of those art deco hotels
in Miami Beach, a little back room on a court
where you could almost be in Cuba or
Costa Rica of the sweet flesh, and
a wooden shack in one of the mosquito marshes
in Manahawkin or the Outer Banks.
I am planning my cup of tea
and my sweet biscuit,
or my macaroni soup
and my can of sardines.
If I spent the morning washing shirts
I would read for two hours
before I slept through the afternoon.
If I walked first, or swam,
I might feel like writing down words

before I went in for coffee, or more hot water.
I will sit on the black rocks
to make my connections,
near the small basin of foam.
I will look at the footprints
going in and out of the water
and dream up a small blue god to talk to.
I will be just where I was
twenty-five years ago,
breathing in salt,
snorting like a prophet,
turning over the charred wood;
just where I was then,
getting rid of baggage,
living in dreams,
finding a way to change, or sweeten, my clumsy life.

Bradley Beach fountain. Photograph © Joseph Paduano.

Bradley Beach, NJ — July 4th

John Pember

We sat on the beach
at the north edge of town,
comfortable in sandchairs
lugged a block from the home of friends,
and positioned ourselves facing south
toward where the fireworks would start.
To our left,
the red running lights
of the port sides of boats
jockeyed up to Asbury Park.
A moment before darkness
I heard behind me the first chuff
of a rocket being launched
and, in the space of a held breath,
the boom as it echoed off boats and piers.

I turned my chair
as the gold of the next rocket
silhouetted a beachful of faces,
expectant and loyally pointed
at their own town's blackness to the south.
But not mine, a stranger's face.
For a half-hour I watched colors
spangle the sky over Asbury Park.

I knew the last rocket had been spent
when I saw the ocean seem to shift —
green starboard lights
sprinting south for position.
I, as loose and rootless as the boats,
turned and joined the crowd at Bradley Beach.

Shark River Inlet

Thomas Reiter

Let the river take it from us,
nothing lasts:

picture tubes whose rare-earth
elements are lost
a neon sign its word broken
someone slammed a storm door
on the tide
labels thrash like a shad run.

Back from the inlet at dawn,
a pushcart's nickel-plated wheels
(rags glass anything the river
goes under the name of) rattle and flash,
fluttering their light into our day
like blank checks.

Horseshoe Crabs

Frank Finale

Belmar, NJ

I fear the crabs, feel their pincers plying my skin,
picking at the mind's flaws.
See that humped horseshoe with tapered spike that seems to float
above the grains and flounce
like a pugilist when poked. Upset it. Stare at the underside

of fright. Legs, jointed like spiders, writhe for webs
of seaweed, rocks and water,
scramble like insects brought to light from underworlds
of damp stones — claws waging
a war with air, a spike carefully wheedling

the wind. Once Paleozoic crawlers, whose armor-
awkward species survived
the dinosaur and war, their shapes lie beached
and form a trail of lost
horseshoes for mud, sand and time to record.

In the shell of night, in the mythy mind, the crabs rule.
Spiny, adept with claws,
they crawl, black-brown, from a dragon-hissing sea of sleep
up to feast on
some forgotten fear; some shape too distant to remember.

Sand Castle Contest: Belmar

Susanna Lippoczy Rich

Finer than gravel, coarser than dust,
this sand, like hope, loves only what crumbles.

We converge — queues of bikinis in SPFs,
Trailways of children in uniform Ts,
hillocks of Santa bellies tanned,
creased white from hunched, unshaded sleep —

and our yellow-shirted Bell Atlantic sponsors
milling like wasps with clipboards and pens,
while McDonald's gold arch startles
in the disemboweled boardwalk pavilion.

We build a wall of screams and scurries
against the breakers,
and haul its small claws of foam
in our complimentary buckets

to mold a momentary clay, moist enough
to shape these effigies of ourselves
that rise from the beach like breaths —
a silent spraypainted boombox of sand,

a half soccer ball, an old convertible
mound and crater and moon the beach.
Those who know sport spray bottles,
and hoses they i.v. into the bellies

of sand sharks and dolphins,
mermaids blinking seashells
against an exacting sun.
Something in having to do this in throngs —

bury our smiling children to the necks,
build castles ringed with Escher stairs,

forsaking the trouble of inner rooms.
Always a struggle between dry and moist,

the inevitable collapse to wind or tide —
these machines of imagination —
sand telephones reaching sand cords
to water that takes no messages.

Trophies, plaques, ten seconds on cable:
small silicate tokens of us —
substance of glass teased from a jealous ocean,
in this no-contest

with precipitates of conches, granulates of bones,
shaped by the grace of not having to last.

Belmar pavilion. Photograph © Joseph Paduano.

The Lessons

Thomas Reiter

Balanced on granite at the point of the jetty,
I watched the beacon from a lightship
anchored where a freighter had broken up.

What was it I had read in that text
open on the table by my sleeping daughter,
forehead pressed to her crossed wrists? —
That an atomic clock can measure
the 1/50,000 of a second lost each year
to tidal friction when the seas bulge
and the earth turns under them.

I picked up a wave in the middle distance,
the beam of the lightship riding it
like a moon-colored version of an algae bloom.

I had crossed the Belmar beach
that mild winter night past someone waving
the pod of a metal detector
over the sand, a flashlight and small bag
for the rings and coins of summer;
past a classic in sneakers and long topcoat,
who could have been on a break
from holding his ear to a water glass
positioned to a wall at the Rocket Motel.
They moved on and now
the wave broke, sealight on stone.

I followed its edge flashing the length of the jetty
and remembered that day in fifth grade
when a nun shut me in the supply room
to trim composition paper. That cold green template
scored into sizes, that blade set up for guilt
because I had given a nickname
to a new classmate, a shy girl

who lived along the stinking slough.
I threw my weight onto the handle
so it brought me down along the pencil line:
the edge-and-whetstone pitch
ending in a boot thump
as margins fell away, piling up in penance.

Light and guidance. Among darkened arcades
along Ocean Avenue was the studio
where I had brought my daughter for her first lesson
in jazz dancing: a figure moving, breaking off
to poise and waver in a soundless timing.

She stood in the doorway and found me
against the lightship, waving.
She crossed the road and descended
past the tideline of mussel shells,
then began going through her steps
along the spine of the jetty,
throwing her arms from side to side
as though flicking water from her fingertips.

What did one name that made a small girl weep
come to after thirty years?
I laughed at myself and began
some castoff ballroom steps,
one arm angled up, the other crooked in front,
sweeping toward my daughter from stone to stone.

She came out of one light dancing,
and I another.
For a moment our weightlessness was made of that.

The Red Rotunda and Its Silver Echo

Jean Hollander

Rising, they drove the mist back to sea,
the red rotunda and its silver echo.
We pursued the unapproachable distance
till the boardwalk ended. Still,
the embarrassment of walking back haunts me.
August rained, deserting the beach.

In autumn we came to Spring Lake
to piece the puzzled map.
The red rotunda overwhelmed us,
cresting a winged hotel. Coldly,
the silver dome removed itself,
luring. That night we reached the base:
Donovan's Penny Arcade.

Should we have climbed the top?
We chose a drive-in. As always,
love conquered while I slept.

Now, another summer drives the fog.
The sky is clean, the red rotunda trimmed
into flat roof of condominiums.
The windblown silver dome
divests itself. At our hotel,
a forties' jazz band plays
to aging dancers, wives arrayed
in lavender prom gowns.
Should we have come?

Weekend at Spring Lake

Maria Mazziotti Gillan

The sea at Spring Lake touches shore,
delicately as a man touching the thigh
of a woman he loves. We watch from the boardwalk
as the sun sets and the moon rises, whispering
as though we are in the presence of something sacred.

Later, we return to the veranda of the old house.
We sit in silence, watching the lights of a ship move
through all that darkness. Above our heads, a net
full of stars and a orange moon, three-quarters full.
We are content to drink clear night air.
Peace, softer than cashmere, settles over us.

Spring Lake pavilion. Photograph © Joseph Paduano.

Seascape: Manasquan, NJ

Frank Finale

Wet shells sheen the beach
splinters of light needling sand and eye.
Gulls sailor waves of breeze
    skim rocks' mussels and glide
        preying over crosses of masts.
To life that tunes its pitch to scales of waves,
the slow sea whistles the rhythm of sun and moon.
        Fiddlers step through sand in time
and broken crabs' claws lie;
between the charred drift they tumbled
    up to shore, teeth to sand.
Brittle as fall's last leaves,
shroud in rags of seaweed,
    rich in decay,
the forests of the sea's dead
lying under indifferent gulls —
wet shells sheening the beach.

Mussels

David Keller

Manasquan, NJ

Each time it's a surprise, finding a shell
on the beach, each one different,
like a childhood, the one that sought you out
without your knowing. How natural it feels
to the hand. I always think
they're white, but this one's dark.
Inside it is a tea-stained tongue,
the soft sound of inlets to the sea
at the tide's running, shallow ripples
and the reflections over the shells like gold,
a man spreading his good fortune
from a leather pouch onto the scale pan,
weighing in the gold to send money home.

In the kitchen are dozens of mussels
with the dirt and rough manners scrubbed off.
We will have them cooked in white wine.
It is impossible, there are so many.
How large the ocean must be,
and the man from the strict plains states
who first came on a hill, an Indian mound
of shells, amazed at these discarded moons,
thousands, an entire history of desire.
After the last one is gone
we will swab our plates with French bread
and sop up the fragrant yellow sauce,
rich and silent in the imagining as gold.

To Joan & Peter & Sylvia Shannon

Manasquan Pizza

Ed Smith

Robert Louis Stevenson wrote
at the Union House after
spending "4 hours in a catboat" but

tonite, pizza slices on the boardwalk fill
everyone's mouth as the stars shine under
a hot hot August orange neon night.

With crazy teenagers laughing, drinking, and
dancing at the Osprey Bar as they beckon as
if tomorrow never arrives on time.

Blues

Alice Friman

"Keep your eyes on the birds,
 the bluefish are just under them."
Shore Times, October 1990

1.
The second week in October
when blues are running strong
in the Manasquan Inlet off the Jersey coast,
we ate bacon and eggs at Duffy's
on the corner, then walked
the shoreline barefoot, watching high tide
gather itself up and gallop in. And you,
never having seen this before, waded in
up to your knees, laughing,
then shimmied in your clothes
like the center of a washing machine
dancing in white foam. The herring gulls arced
and catching at the sun, made their cry.

2.
You troll for blues,
keep the boat moving, the ends of the lines
flashing hammered-metal squid, like silver spoons.
At the rear of the charter, the Sunday crowd
gathers, rummages in make-do boxes, playing with
tackle — their leaders and lures — singing army
songs and forgiving each other's old jokes
in the raucous goodness of men, cold sandwiches
and steamy cups, shoulder gentle against
shoulder in padded layers of clothes.

Above the laughter, the terns and
great black-backed gulls wheel and bluster
as the boat's wake trails a white part
through the sea where the blues comb fast and
high in the water — streak after radiant streak.

Point Pleasant Beach

Madeline Tiger

stocky couples walk
the boards   the boards
shake and creak with
their steps, the March gusts
take off their steady talk
phrase by phrase
no remarkable couplets
or gusty images, no borders
of rhyme or deep wisdom
shaking up the conversations,
they are taking stock
of incidentals, this life
little comings and goings
how families weather,
in the wake of winter
before the seasonal guests
come to the rentals, (just
this, echoing jog in apposition
to the breakers and fine line
of unsmiling Atlantic of
no Amusements, reasonable
briefly) before the boarded up
concessions break down
their cold front barriers to
the waves of cormorants

Point Pleasant Beach boardwalk. Photograph © Joseph Paduano.

On the Boardwalk at Point Pleasant Beach

Frank Finale

A monopoly of summer
cottages lines the north boardwalk
then gives way to gift shops, food stands,
and arcades widening into the heart
of Jenkinson's Pavilion, where games
crackle with light and the perpetual chatter
of push-button weapons blasting cosmic
targets. A wispy, sweet smell of cotton
candy slips through the spicy aroma
of sausage and peppers. Some afternoons,
I sit on a bench near the railing and read
sea poems from a pocket anthology, while the sea
whispers for me to look up and listen
to the real thing. Later, the sand blooms
with beach umbrellas and oil-shined bathers
who rediscover the Jersey shore.
I play Skee-Ball and pinball in arcades
where machines blink away
my quarters in a twinkle of lights.
Or, under a thatched umbrella at Martell's
Tiki Bar, I listen to reggae of No Discipline,
tinkle of ice, laughter of crowd, and hiss-boom
of sea. The waitress serves a parasoled drink.
Dusk deepens. The crowd swells and families sail
into the night, their pockets laden with change.
Inside the boardwalk's new aquarium,
exotic fish glide back and forth
as stars go silently over the ocean.

Machismo

Michael J. Bugeja

for Shane

He watches from the beach, shovel and pail
Abandoned, and begs to accompany
Dad beyond the breakers at Point Pleasant.

I know the undertow, the jellyfish,
The tide. Even the occasional shark.
But not the myriad dangers of love.

Life guards, oiled muscled men, flex on stools.
The waves quell, and my four-year-old cries *please*!
Why not? His life has been a buckle up

Till now: car seats, bike seats, high chairs, boosters.
So I get him, pull straps of his jacket
And skip into calm waters. Mothers shake

Their heads under the rainbow umbrellas.
He wants me to let go the way I would
A two-wheeler so he can bob on waves

As if they were one more amusement ride.
I let him puppy-paddle out to sea.
The wind picks up again, and the rising

Wall picks up my son — slams him into me,
Below/behind and then on top of me —
A tether ball abrading on the sand.

The mothers receive us with their towels
And scowls. My son locates his and leaps from
My arms. There is truth in what he tells her.

"I saved Dad," he says. "Can we go home now?"

Twilight Lake

Frank Finale

reflects this Bay Head morning
smooth and bright as the mute swan
that floats out from
the rushes, reeds, and cattails.
Ducks circle the lake and plash
down, breaking the reflection.
They paddle to where a young
couple and their small girl throw
bits of white bread on the grass.
A little lake of gulls, doves,
mallards, and geese shapes about them,
while damselflies and darning needles
hover and dart above the fragrant
water lilies. Across the avenue,
Victorians and cedarshake cottages
hold vigil over this sanctuary. An artist
sets up his white canvas and begins
to paint what is there, what is not.

Walking the Metedeconk

Thomas Reiter

1.
Soon there'll be a March day
like a double agent,
playing the blue anemone off
against brown umbels of Queen Anne's lace,

but today the only open water
is thin bands around cattails,
so we trust ice with our weight.

2.
You bend to snap off a stalk
because the burst flower sprayed with acrylic
will make a centerpiece —
and suddenly we are on our knees
watching pincers moving armor plate
from the bottom into the light.

Look: In the seed heads of cattails
the backs of stoneflies crack open
onto ginger wings and what passes
for the afterlife.

3.
Wherever we walk, empty-handed,
they are coming down out of the air.
They stipple eggs onto stalks, each
in its ring of water

widening to let us in.

Starfish. Photograph © Joseph Paduano.

Lavallette

John R. Smith

This is the ocean before memory
and those are the pelicans
my grandfather told me
used to pilot the waves before I was born.

I swear that's the same dolphin
that surfaces in my dreams,
and this is the sea glass my sister and I
gathered and polished like gems.

I understand what water means.
I've been thirsty all my life,
but no matter how long it's been,
I've never forgotten how to swim.

I've seen the sea blue, gray, and green,
sharp as a bed of shells
and stellar with jellyfish.
And I've suffered its undertow.

So I take the sand very seriously,
and this year the beach grass
stitched in rows across the young dunes
is a promising binding.

But I know the waves, like pages
in the book of all there is to know,
turn over themselves as they come
and into their own as they go.

Skiff Builder, 1994

Rich Youmans

His shop was a landmark
in Lavallette, and he
had become its legend:
the one who built skiffs
of oak and cedar
cut from the Jersey swamps.

A family craft, handed down
with the chisels and slicks
that were always sharp,
that he used to build
four thousand boats — each one
by hand, by eye. Trained as a boy,
he needed no plan: he knew
in his bones how the grain
should go, could tell
by lifting a plank of cedar
whether it had seasoned right.

Now he was the last,
and he knew that too: far
from the days before fiberglass
when his skiffs could be found up and
down this coast, by lifeguard stands
or in fishing pounds, skimming
over breakers like ducks.
Back when this island
was overrun with rushes,
plum, and bayberry leaves,
boatbuilding was an industry:
each day loud with the busy sounds
of wood becoming something more:
a keel, a slanted transom, a centerboard.

Now lots and their summer cottages
were crowded tight as the planks
of his hulls, and fiberglass was king.
He was the last, and he knew it:
no sons or daughters to pass
his skill, few workers left
who cared. "The demand is gone,"
he would say when asked. "No point
worrying — I had a good time."

Yet a life's work doesn't end easily.
Once he gave a class at the
Seaport Museum, to the few
who had heard and wanted
to learn. He talked, and his fingers
turned familiar again as he guided
younger hands over cedar's long grain:
craft preserved for the sake of craft,
for the sake of knowing it was done.
"No," he told them, over and over,
his voice as blunt as the wood itself,
"like this . . . like this."

City Girls at Seaside Heights

Frank Finale

They will come again this summer, bare-legged
girls with boys under their asses,
to try and grab a piece
of the sun. The rum in their tropical
drinks will blossom their cheeks, their dreams
grow verdant in August; they will move
their tans over the dark cracks
of the boardwalk, to the rhythm of steel
vibrations on dance floors, or behind
the shine of dark glasses and ice-white
smiles. Like salmon running upstream
to spawn, they will flash their tails,
till all their bubble and boil expends
itself leaving plastic bottles and reeds
of straws — the bones of their dollars
and time dissolving on the sand.

Jersey Shore Haiku

Alexis K. Rotella

Seaside Heights, NJ

First trip
to the Jersey shore —
ticky tack.

Down the boardwalk
an old woman pushes
her wheelchair.

In the fun house
my *faux* pearls
scatter.

Carousel children
their faces
a blur.

Seven feet tall
the short-order
cook.

Staring out to sea —
our mouths filled
with taffy.

Seaside Heights boardwalk. Photograph © Joseph Paduano.

On the Boardwalk in Seaside Heights

Martin Jude Farawell

[An excerpt]

A girl in a humid shirt, her sex
as crisp as apples,
intones invitations to a game of chance.
I keep my hands in my pockets,
fingering change, wonder
if I've spent my life
like an old lady with a roll of quarters
in a garish purse,
gambled off bit by bit,
never risking anything that matters.

They slap their money
on the painted counter, stare
as if staring
could conjure the one
that will pluck them out
from the logic of numbers,
the terrible logic
of random necessity.
But all the numbers
that rattle past
the pointing hand
tick down
to that final cipher,
the "O," passive or terrified,
"so this is the day."

River Watch

Frank Finale

Toms River, NJ

The halyards on aluminum masts begin
chinging like little buoys.
Upriver a speedboat buzzes open
a white scar. Sailboats waggle
their masts as though anticipating a wind.
Low lapping sounds reach the bank;
deposit crab claws, driftwood, pebbles, then leave;
return with weeds, shells; leave
with flowers; return. Leave. The sailboats are still,
the river metallic
in scales of light — a chain of mail.
On the river's bank, all .
the houses scintilla the sun, their windows
shrill with light. The brilliance
recedes. The river purls into twilight
and the dark bay of the ocean.

The Fishermen: Island Beach State Park

Frank Finale

The fishermen — ocean wise — watch. Gripped
by the Atlantic, they stand   casting   planting
their poles   against the horizon.   The surf
hissing bright   breaks   coiling around
their boots.   Sundown.   Moonrise.   The beach
a lunar desert.   Hooking into the dark,
they light their driftwood fires.   Wait.
The moon, a phosphorescent glow, hosts their forms.
Hours later, turning to sea again, sun
forsythias the horizon.   On scales
of light, fishermen's pitched figures,
like notes, inherit the music
of this place.   A smell of salt   crystals   the air.

On the Beach

David Keller

Island Beach State Park, NJ

After that argument, I walked off
to bury the sight of her, burn it.
How she must hate, the words like fists
between us and she would not give in.
The hurt, slow surf cut fjords
into the ragged shore and sky,
borders of the country where her anger watched,

its white birds overhead
sharp as insults skimming the water.
Trying to walk that foreign country
beyond the crowds I saw an old boat
ahead of me, one side tipped to show
it must have heaved up
at the land's edge after a storm, filled

with sand. I wanted to turn it to a reward,
some adventure this flat, summer afternoon.
The clear water over the bottom
sparkled, a run of small ripples,
but up close the sides were bare,
porous as old bone, splintered
by difficulties over time and weather.

Once I saw there was nothing
worth taking, I wandered off
past families until the horizon covered them.
At a sudden six tracks
I stopped, the rest washed away,
a gull's, not the sign of some human
company in this salt desert of things lost,

or separated from their cause:
the breeze weeping into the late sun,
the glass of the clear ruined jellyfish
and the ocean's constant Hush, Now Hush.
Returning I found one large clam
on the sand, big as two fists
and still closed though trembling

at the edges like a mouth. I thought
to make a box out of the two halves.
Not sure what use there was
in that, either for myself or her,
and to avoid more cruelty
I threw the animal as far out
toward another chance as I could.

Island Beach State Park

Frank Finale

Once over the high dunes
a rush of light, an expanse of space.
Loose curves of tideline, arcs of gulls
and pale horizon replace
buildings' hard angles,
grids of blocks. Here, waves glitter
a thousand small suns. A herring gull
Kweeeah-ahs like a rusty pulley,
while an osprey whistles its *you you you*
circling toward bayside cedars.
A hollow boom echoes up and
down the shore, a white hiss
of foam — the mantra of the sea.

The long rhythm of the surf in my ears, I step
into the necklace of the tideline:
the clatter and crunch of periwinkles,
scallops, jackknife clams; bits of sponge,
moon shells, a mermaid's purse;
even a gull's skull picked clean by beetles,
its sharp, yellow beak still menacing.
The only prints along wet, darkened sand
are the cuneiform tracks of gulls
and my own. Here, under a sky
the color of salt, my aloneness
grows exquisite as beach glass:
turquoise, amber, emerald. . . .

Island Beach State Park. Photograph © Joseph Paduano.

Ocean Gate

Martin Jude Farawell

Summers used to always smell like this
green stain of fern leaves rolled
to dark moisture between palms,
of soil that puckered open
where garden weeds were plucked,
and shook loose from shaggy-rooted undersides,
of wet seining nets and creosoted piers,
of seaweed-tangled mussels at low tide,
of charcoal and citronella and cat-tail smoke,
of oranges and iced coffee, and peaches in red wine.

And behind the slap of poker cards
against the table top,
and the jingle of penny jars,
crickets scritched their insect lust
as beetles and moths thrummed
at window screens,
and the one that got in pinged
against the light until it died.
And after the long, droning day,
I'd crawl across creaking bed springs
to lie by the open window
where nightbirds called me and
called me and called me

And first up at first light,
I'd wander the woods until noon,
with a bucket for wild blueberries that grew
just beyond the border
of brambles and thorn bushes
that scraped beaded blood paths
across my knees and calves.
And returning to the faces
that had worried away the morning,
would lift up the bucket,

heavy with harvest,
and be forgiven for not being lost
but only gone blueberry picking.

But I was lost.
Lost and wandering after
whatever it was,
in the still summer air,
that scritched at the screens,
that thrummed in panic
against my body,
desperate to get in,
more desperate to get out.
Something — there was so much
I wanted then,
I didn't know what,
only knew when most alone,
under the guise
of blueberry picking,
Would silence tell me
what I listened for.

I am still wandering into summer noons,
after old scents, old sounds, as if one
could open the past for me
and let me find the boy who wanders there
and take his hand, and lead him
to the secret place
of perfect wild berries,
where we pick and eat and laugh and know
this fern scent, this bird cry,
this late fruit breaking
on our tongues.

Piney

Thomas Reiter

An immense river lies below the New Jersey Pine Barrens in aquifers, strata so dense that ground water reaching the Atlantic today fell a few miles inland as rain before the first explorers came.

— News item

He'd never tow a fishing shanty
from public landing onto public ice,
never be a Sears ad in safety colors,
license pinned like a security pass.

Instead, through pine and coastal pepperbush
that would total the game warden's
snowmobile, he forces a foot route,
setting traplines and crossbow fishing
always now on posted land —
why else would anyone be
a fifth-generation Piney?

Hidden from the cranberry farms
where men climb into waders
and steer threshers like garden tillers
bobbing on pontoons — all
to make that water blaze
and vacuum it black again —
he knows bogs along Cedar Creek
so rich in tannic acid
that nothing in them changes.
Any one might stare him down
with the face of the Jersey Devil, that
13th child of a 13th child,
drowned at birth. Somewhere

between Lanoka Harbor and Pinewald,
where springs from that aquifer
sifting through clay
pare the ice for arrows,

he waits, knowing how any April
midges could be sawdust dancing on a plank
as a ripsaw passes through it.

He does not look up from target ice
that fell 500 years ago
as a summer shower in the wilderness.
He releases line
spooled at his waist, and in his palm
takes the turn of the crossbow's throat.

Lucky's Soliloquy
on the Death of the Eel Potter

Nicholas Delo

When we found him
he was out past the point,
out past Ronny's duck blind,
past the osprey nests,
out near the farthest edge
of Cedar Creek, where
the state had cut the marsh
into long parallels, dredged
mosquito ditches, row after
row, in hopes of pulling
more bait-fish off the bay.
That's where we found him,
the gaunt old man, half fallen
over one of his own eel pots —
the eels inside long since
dried up like leathery twigs;
and at his side was his burlap sack,
filled with the broken bits
of horseshoe-crab,
with oyster halves,
with little necks, and scallops,
and the unused hunks
of bunker and mullet
and blues he had collected
from the line trawlers
down on the docks,
all of it tied up
in that big heavy sack of his,
all of it, as if, after
six decades of potting
and trapping and skinning
this is what he'd bring.
God's honest truth,
this is what he'd bring.

Barnegat Bay. Photograph © Ray Fisk.

3 a.m., Barnegat Bay

Nicholas Delo

From our back deck, I can see
the boys down on the dock. The three
of them are walking, balanced atop
the farthest edge of bulkhead,

their arms outstretched with
buckets and rods and small white
cartons of grass-shrimp, and although
they're headed out near the end

of the yard, out towards the slip
where Tunnelson keeps his old garvey,
they sound as if they could be right here,
standing next to me. You should be here.

You should hear this. It's amazing,
you know, the way the lagoon does that to you —
amplifies everything. The faint clank
of an anchor. The ropes tightening

and creaking around pilings.
A telephone on the opposite shore.
The conversation somewhere,
in someone's kitchen.

Patroling Barnegat
Walt Whitman

Wild, wild the storm, and the sea high running,
Steady the roar of the gale, with incessant undertone muttering,
Shouts of demoniac laughter fitfully piercing and pealing,
Waves, air, midnight, their savagest trinity lashing,
Out in the shadows there milk-white combs careering,
On beachy slush and sand spirts of snow fierce slanting,
Where through the murk the easterly death-wind breasting,
Through cutting swirl and spray watchful and firm advancing,
(That in the distance! is that a wreck? is the red signal flaring?)
Slush and sand of the beach tireless till daylight wending,
Steadily, slowly, through hoarse roar never remitting,
Along the midnight edge by those milk-white combs careering,
A group of dim, weird forms, struggling, the night confronting,
That savage trinity warily watching.

Barnegat Light

Jeanne Marie Beaumont

A quarter century has passed
since the big hurricane slashed
this isle in two, launched houses into
Manahawkin Bay and severed
cedars from their sandy roots.

It's all been healed. Riding north
on my Raleigh three-speed bike
there's a plethora of signboards.
Even the stiff fishbone branches
of scrub pine have been bought and planted.

They look enlarged this year, the land-
scape's new design is rich with green —
planned privacy now every plot
of sand shifts into building lots
for the anxious real-estate brigands.

A few Victorians still stand,
where captains bedded between fleets;
stalwart before the century's onslaughts,
they collect the standard legends,
dogged renovators, ghosts.

The town sprawls at the island's tip:
Old Barney, through with warning ships,
hoists tourists for a gull's-eye view;
a Dairy Queen, marine supply
and Coast Guard station anchor the bay.

Beyond that, just a leaning row
of seamen shacks. This season it's
been purged of its "Viking Village"
merchandise; all mute, doors barred,
it rots, waiting to be landmarked.

As I turn around, a wall of wind
confounds each pedal's thrust. Knees strained,
thighs sore, I plod southward with sweaty hands
and curse this fact I should accept
by now, so often I have coasted

along this graveled radius,
heedless in my ease how fast
or far I've come. Right to this island's end
I ride deceived, so great the force
of wind flung at my back.

Barnegat Lighthouse. Photograph © Ray Fisk.

The Sea Beyond the Breakers
(Barnegat Light, NJ, 1980)
William J. Higginson

Shipwrecks are apropos of nothing.
If men could only train for them
and have them occur when the men
had reached the pink of condition,
there would be less drowning at sea.
from "The Open Boat"
Stephen Crane

The Atlantic was my first water, the waves at Montauk Point
bobbing me up and down, a frog of an infant one lucky summer day.
But I was twelve before I finally learned to swim, and that
in fresh water, a sharp jump from a dock into cold so cold
it took a while to realize it was water, and stroke back up
the fifteen or twenty feet I'd gone down. From then on, I swam.
I never much liked man-made pools, though I have done some laps,
but always hungered for a lake, a clear pool in a mountain stream,
a place where trees connect the sky and water, where the limit
is approachable, and swimming is a means of transportation,
a way of getting from here to the other side, to the dock or boat
that offers rest or sun or fellowship after the lovely singularity
of floating over, cutting under the water, bursting up into air
that knew no other purpose than filling the sweet ache in my chest.

When, in my twenties, I came again to the sea, it was Pacific,
the blue Pacific on the north coast of Honshu, Japan's main island.
The beach was empty and stretched for miles that summer, all sand
and flat, no dunes to separate it from the trees that swayed
a hundred yards or so from the low-tide water's edge.
The strange customs of swimming and sun-bathing had not yet come
to this part of Japan. Occasionally one or two Japanese
would walk the beach, gathering driftwood for their fires.
The water was poisoned, according to some persistent rumor
circulating on the American military base I'd come from,
and as I sat in the shade of the trees at the beach's edge
I saw an Air Force helicopter patrolling along the coast,
a hundred feet or so above the white-capped breakers.

Timed to avoid the patrol, a few furtive dips amounted more
to splashing in the breakers ankle or waist deep than swimming.

After I came home from Japan and met my strange wife and child,
my mother took the three of us for a vacation to Cape May,
to enjoy the October beach, to get to know one another.
The leaden grey breakers reminded me of typhoon-whipped waves
breaking against the north Pacific sea-wall at Wakkanai, Japan.
I swam gloriously in them, protected by the jetty holding back
the worst the north Atlantic offered on that sunny day,
my wife lounging on the sand, wondering what crazy man this was
who swam in the October sea as our daughter filled a pail with sand.
I left that marriage, which was more an absence than a presence,
and now after ten years alone I have married my maiden of the sea,
a girl whose childhood summers rocked in the waves at Barnegat,
who lost her silver bracelet to the sea and waits for its return.

In August, when the heat had reached its height, we came
to Barnegat again, to forget all save the ocean and the sun.
We walked slowly into the water; it cooled us as it threw us
in the ever-changing-never-ending roll of surf upon the beach.
I swam out, past my wife, toward the younger swimmers
who angled themselves into a wave and were carried in its curve
to grope for footing, splashing in the foam as it hit the beach.
Their exercise was love; this foaming lover carried them boldly,
swiftly to the beach, then disappeared, to rise again out there,
beckoning them to return, to repeat the dance of plunging through
and riding swiftly back. But I was after calmer things.
For I had swum across a lake or two, knew the peace of open sky
whose only limit was the small trees on a distant, curving shore.
But I had never swum beyond the breakers, into the greater curve
of the ocean draped around the earth, and wished to know the rise
and fall of swells, not waves and breakers casting up on sand.

I pushed through the last wave rising toward the beach

and kept on going. A long, slow undulation raised me up.
I turned and slid slowly into a deepness between the swells
and could not see the beach. Treading water again I rose
and now I saw it, far away, no person recognizable. My wife
had waved before I broke through the last crest coming out,
but now I could not distinguish her, and gave up trying.
The swimmers on the other side of the first white caps
were slowly growing smaller, as the sun-glinted water carried me
further from shore, and the beach became a narrow strip of tan
and green against the sky.

        I was too far out, and didn't know
if I could make it back. The life-guard stand gleamed red
up on the beach, sloping slightly toward the water where I was.
I wondered if they'd see me if I waved, and come to drag me in.
Well, I can get in, I thought, and began to stroke the same calm,
powerful strokes that had taken me past the breakers at the start.

    But I was tired, and these strokes were not the same.
    I did not have the power that I had had before,
    and seemed to make no headway toward the beach,
    toward the group of noisy swimmers just beyond
    the breakers I had crossed, some twenty yards away.
    And now I really wasn't sure that I could make it,
    and changed from the familiar stroke and glide
    of my favorite breast stroke to a lunging crawl,
    the clumsiest and least efficient of my strokes.
    I felt the water hauling me out, away from the beach,
    and quickly gave that up. Rolling over on my back,
    I considered the sky, and whether I would review my life.

Apparently I was not due to die, for I could not remember it, any
part of it, and was left with the job of getting back to the beach.
Rolling over into a comfortable over-arm side-stroke I slid
slowly through the water between me and the group of noisy ones,

gratefully felt the spray of a breaker crash over my head,
and realized how much work still lay before me: I was too tired
to ride the breakers in. So I swam until I could touch bottom,
testing the depth every few strokes, until I gained a toe-hold
on the sand, and was washed quickly off my feet by the next wave.
And still I could not rest, but had to swim to stay afloat
in the crashing waves.

        When at last I could stand without falling,
and walked free of the curling spray, my wife came to me.
Her worried look told me she knew that I'd been too far out,
and she told me how the life-guard had watched me from the edge
of the life-guard stand, grabbed his float even, and been ready
to come and get me had I floundered in the waves, or raised a hand.
With my arm over her shoulder, we walked out of the last shallow water
and up to the life-guard stand, up to the young blond-headed man
who'd kept his eye on me that last half hour, who now looked out
at others playing in the sea, and thanked him for being ready
to come and get me had I floundered in the waves, or raised a hand.
He smiled and praised me for not panicking, for floating on my back,
then said: 'Yeah, there's quite a rip-tide out there, we had
twenty-five saves out here yesterday.' We thanked him again,
and walked to where our blanket and towels lay on the beach
as I welcomed the thought that I was not one of twenty-five saves,
or worse.

    I suppose there is a pride in coming back,
but the lesson learned is more important
than any pride for getting back myself.
The self that took me out there still would swim,
and bides its time until another wave will beckon.

4th Street Pond at Dawn, Barnegat Light Inlet

Mary C. Bilderback

A black skimmer works the cove.
He goes in low, beak angled deep
Into the sky-drenched water,
Slitting the seam between two worlds.

This is not a man-made pond.
You can tell by the rocks,
And the ducks in the middle
Counting their feathers.

A fish bumps the surface.
A raindrop jumps from a storm cloud overhead.
Rings of water like a conversation
Fill and break each other.

A cormorant hangs up its wings to dry.
A willet wakes.
Red legs scratch brown heads.

Five O'Clock Terns: Loveladies, LBI

Jeanne Marie Beaumont

After weeks of seeing only one or two,
out of the blue of four directions
a flock of terns gathers,
black-tailed formality in a high mass.

Bent airbrushed wings skim overhead
all angling toward the meeting spot.
They land as on command and plump
as their grey wings are tucked.

They stake their sand, starch-white
bellies glinting late-day sun,
turning the hoods of their jetblack heads —
a convention of executioners.

And who's to say they're not?
One by one they swoop toward the ocean
with a shrill ca-caw. Pumping the damp air,
they dangle over the low sea
like an unfinished sentence.

At the Seashore: Loveladies

Jean Hollander

My body curled around an aching tooth,
With borrowed pen inept in midnight hand
In father's script, too large for words
I write upon a page of night.
Darkly I hear them breathe
Frail emblem of a man and purloined child,
Collage of us and ancestors unknown.
Behind the curtain, in her sleep, she sighs.
The shuttered windows shriek against the tide,
Venetians bang the wind our island rides.
Like silverfish the shadows glide
Into my coral flesh.

    amavi   amo   amabo

Upon our balcony I stop the night.
The wind has calmed. Gently
The island nods against its bridge.
A ball of gnats glides through the silent air.
Far from the dawn a seagull cries
And I remember porpoises at noon
Midway in mist from sand to edge of blue
Seemed sharks to landed fears until
In foaming curve from sea to sky
They luminous leaped and dived and leaped again
Their joyous, aimless, iridescent game.

Summer storm over Barnegat Bay, Long Beach Island. Photograph © Ray Fisk.

Lady Moonlight of Long Beach Island

Geraldine C. Little

Unable to sleep I walked onto the beach
at Ship Bottom. Midnight. No one there. Windless
hot night, bright with the full moon's elegant reach
across moderate waves, seaweeds, shell-littered sands.
A driftwood log offered its essence for seat,
so I sat. One shouldn't refuse any thing's self.
How intimate the stillness, accentuated by the beat
of vocal waves. Was it they who'd summoned me here?

Suddenly I stood, squinting along the lane
of light to a sailing ship that seemed to be sinking.
A *sailing ship*. I must be dreaming, insane,
a bit. Perhaps moon-touched? No sailing ships
like that anymore. Then, like a projected
slide changed to the next, it disappeared
leaving the road empty, silently glimmering.
Should I race for help? Indecision quivered dry lips.

Next moment, lovely as a lily at Easter, she came
moving on moonlight, long skirts the color of moon,
bedraggled, weighted with water, long hair like rain,
that silvery, flying behind her. In *no* wind!
Nearer, nearer. Voice pitched low as a cello
she spoke (not to me, to air), desperately:
Where did they bury my jewels, my treasure, my all?
This beach? These dunes? Her heart seemed graved with the rune.

Slowly I walked towards her, no fear in my bones
for so anguished a lady. *What ship was that*, I asked.
Did THEY take your treasure? (Had I glimpsed skull & crossbones
before the sinking?) I stretched out a tentative hand
and touched only moonflushed air in the shape of nothing.
Nothing, I whispered, backing to floodlit log
become cold, its essence unwelcoming, masked.
A mirage? Pale as the moon, I dazed to bed.

What *is* a mirage, exactly? I read definitions
defining nothing I saw or heard — or saw
again, next summer, by Barnegat Light. Again
a sleepless span for me, and a sort of summoning
to the pier crowded in daylight with tourists, fishermen.
Floating round the Light, in light, she came
wearing her cries like gone-time garments, raw,
cold in the summer night, sadly beseeching,

and beyond her, sinking to depths, the sailing ship.
I moved again towards her sorrow, couldn't touch it.
(Can you ever touch sorrow?) Again my hands found nothing
but luminosity that offered no light on it all.
What *is* mirage? I tell no one these visions,
knowing how people scoff at visions. Each summer,
since, I've seen her, searching and beautiful, embodiment
of nothing I understand. But I love her, lovely

mystery inherent in seaweeds, grasses, sands
that shift, change, but never reveal. My Lady.

Surfman No. 7

Ray Fisk

Long Beach Island

I knew this much: the surfman
was from this beach.
His station and number engraved on the bronze tag he wore
so the body could be identified.

I put it in a pocket of my shorts and walked the afternoon tide.
I put the shield on the sand, covering it a little, as if I had just found
this artifact.

As if it could transport me back to this beach a century ago.

Couldn't I smell the odor of Station No. 17
of the United States Lifesaving Service in winter:
sweat, and salt, and damp wool and woodsmoke
inside the clapboard walls packed with eelgrass.

And unspoken fear of the peril of this beach in a big blow —
a nor'easter —
before weather channels and satellites told us how to feel
about storms.

Before this barrier island had been bulldozed
and filled a thousand times over.
Paved, piling-ed, built upon, and landscaped by so many
suburbanites
it had really become the same place
they were racing down the Parkway to leave behind.

Surfman No. 7 knew the uncivilized beach: sideways rain,
sand grit on the teeth and in the eyes, hard surf,
and the wreck's heavy timbers creaking, groaning, splintering.
The suburbanites were oblivious.

I showed my friend
the lifeguard this tag
and I told him the story.
And he said, cool, that's what I am:
A Surfman.
A Surfman of the 1990s.

Landfill, Long Beach Island

Claire C. Beskind

A quiet marsh as reeds
quiver to salt-lapped sea beats;
sanctuary for sparrows, gulls,
and an occasional crane asleep
standing on one spindly leg.

Last fall, in spite of law,
bulldozers appeared with
autumn's steely winds.
Only one woman cried outrage;
grabbed a sluggish turtle
from machine's jaw, beat
her fists against thick steel,
to cry outrage at the burial
of sandpipers' nests,
firmly rooted prickle bushes,
sea-wormed shells of dead mollusks,
at the loss of a sea arm.

Finally others heard
awakened to the law
and now determined reeds return
between puzzled egrets
and tiny eager martins.

Heavy surf, Long Beach Island. Photograph © Ray Fisk.

On the Island

Gerald Stern

Long Beach Island

After cheating each other for eighteen years
this husband and this wife are trying to do something with the three
days they still have left before they go back to the city;
and after cheating the world for fifty years these two old men
touch the rosy skin under their white hair and try to remember
the days of solid brass and real wood
before the Jews came onto the island.
They are worried about the trees in India
and the corruption in the Boy Scouts
and the climbing interest rate,
but most of all they spend their time remembering
the beach the way it was in the early thirties
when all the big hotels here were shaped like Greek churches.

Me, I think about salt
and how my life will one day be clean and simple
if only I can reduce it all to salt,
how I will no longer lie down like a tired dog,
whispering and sighing before I go to sleep,
how I will be able to talk to someone
without going from pure joy to silence
and touch someone
without going from truth to concealment.

Salt is the only thing that lasts on this island.
It gets into the hair, into the eyes, into the clothes,
into the wood, into the metal.
Everything is going to disappear here but the salt.
The flags will go, the piers,
the gift shops, the golf courses, the clam bars,
and the telephone poles and the rows of houses and the string of cars.

I like to think of myself turned to salt
and all that I love turned to salt;
I like to think of coating whatever is left
with my own tongue and fingers.
I like to think of floating again in my first home,
still remembering the warm rock
and its slow destruction,
still remembering the first conversion to blood
and the forcing of the sea into those cramped vessels.

The Goons Are Leaving

Gerald Stern

Long Beach Island

The goons are leaving, and the Hawaiians, and the taffy-pullers,
and the charred wives, and the blackmailers:
this is their Labor Day, the feast of wages.
Only the insolvents are left, and the waifs, and the vagrants.
For one more week we will move through the loose sand
in simple luxury.
We will walk into the sanctuaries and turn the signs;
we will pick our way through the wreckage;
we will start fires;
we will lie in the sun.
At night we will walk the 127 miles in peace.
We will shake the bones of the Unamis and the Presbyterians.
We will sit in the Mansion of Health.
We will rid ourselves of the consining insects.
We will smell the old meadows.
We will undress in the cedars.
We will meet raven on the beach.
Only money and luck have made us different from the others.
We live in grief and ecstasy.
It is our justice.

Running Aground

Shirley Warren

We know Great Bay, the Mullica
River, the local creeks, and all
the surrounding waters as well
as we know our names, and still
from time-to-time we run aground.
Last week it happened because
we were both sitting with our backs
to the cabin, feet toward the stern,
sipping wine. The time before that,
I was reaching over the starboard
hull, trying to pluck a handful
of sea lavender from the riverbank,
and he — my husband, the captain —
had his eye on what he thought was
a corpse, but turned out to be some
ordinary cluster of cabbage and logs
drifting on the tide. We're just not
attentive enough, I understand
from our friends, and I can live
with that. It's simply symptomatic,
a reflection of how we manage
our daily marriage. I'm looking
one way, he another — neither of us
caring where the ship ends up, or what
kind of detritus we'll have to dig
out of to get it afloat again.

Lull

H. A. Maxson

The rivers flow finally out
into the bowl of harbor,
the last hundred feet still orange
with the sweetening rust
of cedar. A single boat,
its sails luffed, waits.
Waves are flat between tides.
Two gulls rise like a colon
as if to announce the next event:

This was the pirates' playground
once, their swift rigs backed
down the throats of the Batsto
and Oswego — waiting.
They dipped river water
to splash with rum
while storms blocked off the coast.
Clippers, sick for the comfort
of land, angled into shoals
deadly with sandbars. They swamped,
then listed, great legless
land beasts, hulls split
until ballast and cargo
spilled like entrails.
Out of river mouths pirates came
taking only fingers captive
when the dead swelled
around their rings.

But today I walk this lip
of sand, sidestepping ridges
of flotsam, the small,
numberless dead, whitening.
When I crouch for treasure
and stare into blades of sun,

I pray for young girls
to emerge from clam shells,
or someone to nail
a doubloon to this blue day.

His Daughter

Shirley Warren

Galloway Township, NJ

On bays that edge our township, where real
rum-runners and pirates angled their ships
through the night, I fish for food these days,
for whatever dull pleasure a closed mouth
might gather, wedged between meaningless
speeches. My father grew up on these
waters, catching eels, digging clams,
rigging sails of his clothing the time he lost
his oars, chasing glimpses of *monstrous*
creatures no one had seen before. One time,
I hear him begin again, he and his brother
were dragged out to sea, by a shark
they'd sunk their anchor in and couldn't
get undone. The tales he's told, and keeps
telling, never seem repetitious. Though I know
that boy at the start of his life had little
idea of *daughter*, he belongs to me now, and
I to him. I anchor myself in these waters.

Egrets, Edwin B. Forsythe National Wildlife Refuge. Photograph © Ray Fisk.

Walking the Marshland

Stephen Dunn

Brigantine Wildlife Refuge, 1987

It was no place for the faithless,
   so I felt a little odd
walking the marshland with my daughters,

Canada geese all around and the blue
   herons just standing there,
safe, and the abundance of swans.

The girls liked saying the words,
   gosling,
egret, whooping crane, and they liked

when I agreed. The casinos were a few miles
   to the east.
I liked saying craps and croupier

and sometimes I wanted to be lost
   in those bright
windowless ruins. It was early April,

the gnats and black flies
   weren't out yet.
The mosquitoes hadn't risen

from their stagnant pools to trouble
   paradise and to give us
the great right to complain.

I loved these girls. The world
   beyond Brigantine
awaited their beauty and beauty

is what others want to own.
   I'd keep that
to myself. The obvious

was so sufficient just then.
   Sandpiper. Red-wing
blackbird. "Yes," I said.

But already we were near the end.
   Praise refuge,
I thought. Praise whatever you can.

Fall Migration at Brigantine

Don Colburn

Instinct is just a word for comings and goings
we can't explain. November brings snow geese
to where the Jersey shore begins or ends,
this unison of marshgrass and mudflats.
And we too have come, a busful
up from the Smithsonian
in boots, plaid hats and binoculars,
our own brand of protective coloration,
eager for a peek at a green-winged teal
among the pintails, or a great blue
fishing from his standstill in the shallows.
We hadn't gone two blocks when someone
checked off *rock dove* and *ring-billed gull.*
Now a coot stalks the mudbank on galoshy feet
while redtails and turkey vultures
kettle high and slow along the thermals.
Across the bay the casino skyline rises
bluish in the haze. There are thresholds
everywhere but no clear lines:
land and water, fresh and salt, wilderness
and honkytonk. A season, this,
for crossing-over: Tundra swans come
and snow geese by thousands down from the Arctic
turn mudflats to a white shimmer. Look!
Another flock, high enough for twilight,
glittery wingbeats trembling the dark sky,
willed south by wind, shoreline, loss
of light, and ancient pulls we nearly remember —
we who have gathered to watch
and call them by name.

At the Noyes Museum: Fall Migration

H. A. Maxson

Three tolls south on the Garden State,
twenty minutes hugging the jag of shoreline —
then sand-road, bull-pine, Canada Geese
at the equinox. The air was white with them
against Atlantic City's blueprint of fog.

The Noyes' new clapboard aged smoke gray
with sun and salt and wind in just a year.
Gulls splashed macadam walks with piss-clams
and thin-shelled mussels, then pecked them clean.
Inside a century's salvage of decoys posed:

shorebirds on wood or wire legs, Mallards
and Buffleheads huddled wingless in their hunched
disguise of sleep. When I opened the blue-glass door,
Canadas and Snow Geese lurched away. The bolt clicked.
Their V shot south, and it was silent as a church.

The Bottom Feeders

Shirley Warren

for my sister Donna, fishing in Absecon Bay

Whether the fish we're after are wary of the barbed
hooks we hang our bait on, we cannot say.
We'd rather surmise a multitude of flounder lying
along the bottom, snuggled in mud and two eyes
up, foolish enough to feed on the squid-draped
minnows we've threaded onto our hooks.
They smell the squid, Daddy used to teach us,
and feel the minnow squiggle. That's why
all our lives we've doubled up on the bait
and patiently waited — lately, it seems, to a fault:
Either the fish aren't biting or they're slipping off
undetected; even as our husbands have burrowed deep
underground, one by one, to relish their midlife
crises. Now the children we brought out of the coziest
warmth our bodies could muster have learned so much
about cold survival *they* "make allowances" for us now.
Snapping our wrists, casting into the wind, we send
our tackle down and settle back to evaluate our drift.
When the tide is right and the breeze agrees, we glide
out of Crosstides like a couple of swans . . . out of Crosstides,
up along the marshes, right past Mankiller Island.
A really good drift lasts forever. We don't
want it to end, we never want it to end. Everything
we took on promised such a good drift, when it began.
Everyone we loved was so hungry for us and our beautiful
bait. I won't be the one to say what went wrong. But notice
how we rig our reels with thicker line these days,
and we're stocking our pockets with heavier hooks.

For a Bottlenosed Dolphin
off the New Jersey Coast
Penny Harter

You can see the lungs of your mate begin to fill.
Does she, twisting her head on its muscled torso,
notice the first signs of the plague
that has already taken so many?
You both have watched it again and again,
slow suffocation,
skin peeling to raw abcess,
the growing weakness,
until they wash up on the shore,
dead or dying.

"It won't happen to us,"
you said to one another,
grieving together in the dark water.
"We have been too happy."

But here it is,
the shadow of fluid rising in her lungs
to drown her;
the fever, the chills, her listless body.

You want to be next.
You follow her, coming in close to the shore.
When you call she cannot answer.

Humans bend over the bodies of your kin,
probing, trying to help.
They carry her away from you,
her breath still bubbling unevenly.
You fear they cannot stop the plague.
You know you will never see her again.

Your children have followed you,
and your friends who are left
wait out beyond the breakers.
Still, you linger in the shallows.
The humans run up and down the beach.
You watch their lungs,
the pumping of their hearts.

Stranded bottlenosed dolphin, August 1988. Photograph © Ray Fisk.

Half-bank, Absecon Creek

Shirley Warren

When I could tell the time
by tides, and sense the first
bright edge of the moon
before it broke across
the ocean's farthest line,
I knew better than now
how it felt to be brave.

Sometimes I stole away
from home in a neighbor's
boat, or simply floated
down the creek on my back,
feeling myself complete
as the shorebirds, waving
my body as I thought
a dolphin might, with grace
and uncommon vigor.

If, at times, the tide
was falling, and sleek, black
mud edged the creek — the time
of day and night I knew
as *half-bank* — my courage
waned. For then I could see
the least beautiful side
of the waters, crawling
with life steeped in decay,
and too slippery for me
to ever scramble out.

But mostly I drifted
out on a rising tide,
with laughing gulls and terns
riding the waves I made.
If I did this when moon-
light was missing, loons
released their mournful
calls to mark my passage.
And I was not afraid.

Blackbeard Returns to Atlantic City

Barbara Helfgott Hyett

This beach used to be a sponge of woods.
Now I can't find an oak to crouch behind.
White mountains of dunes gone
to brick. The cedar swamp is dry.
The new topography: a skin of bungalows,
avenues named for oceans. At every turn
electricity: along the boardwalk,
fishing pavilions and amusement piers,
on the roof garden of the Grand Hotel:
candescence distilled like a swig of rum.

I have come to watch ships sink.
In twenty-two minutes, in a cloud of steam,
yacht *Crystal* burns to the water line.
This is the attraction — five hundred wrecks
before the lighthouse, and it was my light,
my lantern trick that lured them, piled them
five high on the strand in a single night.
I took them in fog, or in the dead of winter,
the sea all spanker and timber, fruit boats,
bunches of green bananas floating frozen,
bags of coconuts rolling in like dice.

I trace the circlings of a cormorant
who spies, with one long eye, my island.
I know there's something buried here —
garnets, silver bullion, a holly forest
just below the sand.

The Keeper of the Light

Barbara Helfgott Hyett

When he dreams, all sound is the voice of water.
Like a man in the drag of sleep, he listens
to the crash on the shoals, waves, the lost
Powhatan, the *Frankfort*, the schooner *Nile*.
The keeper of the light has no secrets.
He has closed the logbooks of ships,
accounted for cargo and the passengers who
drowned. In his room he studies clouds.

He has engineered nothing.
His house was built by someone else:
two hundred steps that fan and spiral,
ten thousand bricks. Ten thousand storms,
the sea as hard as chrysolite.
The keeper of the light is marooned.

Sand rebuilds itself. A city grows
around him. The coast is driftwood,
rancor, and spume. The keeper
doesn't notice. Every morning
he gathers baskets full of birds —
wild ducks, geese, sandhill cranes,
stunned or dead at the base of his tower.

At dusk, birds slam against the white
and banded side, blind, maddened
by the light twirling
in the heartache, the din of wings.

Hudson Fish Market and Absecon Lighthouse, Atlantic City, New Jersey, 1973.
Photograph © George Tice.

Climbing the Lighthouse

Barbara Helfgott Hyett

I'd expected the smell of the sea.
At every landing, arched vaults,
mullions, casements piercing the wall.
I do not lift my eyes,
do not break the stride of climbing
two hundred twenty-eight steps
to the catwalk, railings
thick with rust.
I am grateful for the shadows.

Twelve more steps, helical
and narrow to the lightroom.
I have to inch up sideways,
into the light itself.
Windows reflect the image
of windows. I stare
at the empty reservoir,
imagine gravity
changing the speed of clockwork.

I used to come to Lighthouse Park
to sit all afternoon under the bushes,
watching ants.
Why have I come this time
compelled to climb the stairs,
to circle the diamond latticework?

I wait for something in the shade
to uncover me, to spill me
like seeds.

Nothing Truly Terrible Ever Happened to Me

Shirley Warren

[An excerpt]

I remember thinking those words
ten years ago, when a little boy
slipped out of his father's arms
and into the sea
forty feet below
the Steel Pier.
I remember, too,
when my daughter was that little,
I never held her up to look
over any ledge or sill
unless she was harnessed to my wrist,
and even then my husband
locked his fists
around my waist to anchor us.

My father walked me
to the sandbar in Grassy Channel once.
The whole time we fished,
he fussed about the tide.
If he hadn't — had he let the tide
surprise us — we might have been
stranded there, drowned
like the sandbar itself, our hair
streaming down the incoming current
like angel-grass.

A Game of Monopoly in Chavannes

Maxine Kumin

[An excerpt]

. . . In my mind

I've landed on Boardwalk again and cannot pay,
the Bank is cheating me blind, it's the late thirties.
Too young to do sums, I am almost always in tears.

My brothers, two cousins and I, unaware
we are sent here each summer out of filial duty
squabble over St. James Place and the Short Line

in our grandmother's fusty Atlantic Avenue flat.
From Oma's front room overlooking the Boardwalk
we can hear the surf break and sigh sucking back

but we're unaware of the irony of place:
cheap haven for the Depression's pensioners.
To us Atlantic City is paradise

except when it rains like this, except when we hear
Oma's foreign words that speak pain and terror.
We buck up to decide whose turn to roll the dice

on the massive bleached oak table scrubbed with lemon
its six carved legs ending in jungly claws. . .

Atlantic City 1939

Maxine Kumin

When I was young and returning from
death's door, I served as chaperone,
pale as waxworks, a holiday child,
under the bear laprobe in the back
of my courtesy uncle's Cadillac
careening through a world gone wild.

The Germans pushed into Poland. My
mother sat up front, close pressed
as bees to honey to Uncle Les
and wobbled the stick he shifted by.
I whooped my leftover cough but said
no word, a bear asleep or dead.

Later, in the Boardwalk arcade
when a chirping photographer made
me put my face in the hole with wings,
they snuggled behind him, winked and smiled
as he fussed and clicked the shutter's spring
and there I was corporeal
in the garb of the angel Gabriel,
forever a captive child.

Pink with ardor, not knowing why,
I longed for one of them to die
that slow September by the sea.
He fell on the beach at Normandy.
I never heard her say his name
again without a flush of shame
for my complicity.

Steel Pier 1962

Sandra E. Lundy

any day
at Steel Pier
you could watch
the blonde woman
in the red sequined bathing suit
coax the white horse
off the diving board
Splash! over
and over

then run the splintery
boardwalk
to the velvet brocade movie house
where Boris Karloff
stared straight at you
from the screen,
his white lab coat smeared with blood,
his hideous, cold eyes appraising
the value of your separate parts

afterwards, if you were
in the mood for a little
show-biz entertainment, you could
stroll into Tony Grant's Stars
of Tomorrow Revue,
where The Next Shirley Temple,
in a fringed golden tutu
sang about Daddy
and lollipops

if you were brave enough
you'd ride the diving bell
ten feet to the bottom of the ocean
or twirl in the whirl-a-gig
without screaming

you could smash into your enemies .
on the bumper cars
you could liquefy yourself
in the hall of mirrors

all this for a quarter: the world
as you would come to know it.

High-Diving Horse rider Marion Hackney emerges from Steel Pier Water Circus pool on the back of Dimah (Steel Pier owner Hamid spelled backwards). Photograph courtesy of Vicki Gold Levi Collection.

Steel Pier, Atlantic City

John Grey

It's a fire you take with you,
burning like the devil in your gut,
in your thoughts.
Everything, even years, go up in smoke,
out there, let loose from the Boardwalk,
the swell of water and flames eyeing each other
through the crumpling steel,
the falling debris,
the heat cocking a bright orange snout
at an unsuspecting Summer
and then swallowing it whole.
There goes the Marine Ballroom
with its amazing dance floor
and the Ocean Stadium,
home of the diving horses, Dimah and Gamal,
and the carousel, and the Ferris wheel,
and the memories,
seemingly dry and unwary
brittle as kindling,
like Ronald Harrison,
50 year old half-Sioux Indian
who spent forty-two days
in a six-foot-long concrete coffin
and Tony Bennett
grafting himself onto the melody
silky smooth
and Frank Fontaine slapping sloppy humor
around his twisted mouth
splashing it in giddy faces
and Woody Herman's Band
raking a generation or more
across those jazzy coals
and the Three Stooges
slapsticking their way
up and down aisle after aisle

of rocking seats
even Ricky Nelson
sweetening acne into adoration
and the Rolling Stones
rumbling the wooden beams so hard
the ocean floor almost cracked
and what about Joan Weber warbling
"Let Me Go Lover,"
as if fire lets anything go,
especially not lovers,
the dreams floating high
into the dark night air,
hovering atop the ashes
but choking on the smoke.

Rio Station

Kyle Laws

a cheese steak with fried onions & mushrooms
at 11PM off the island of Wildwood   sitting
in a booth above the dance floor   a band
belting out Judy Collins "Someday Soon"   they
are country western line dancing   a man in a
black Stetson & a woman in a full short skirt
western dancing in my home by the sea   singing
of a young man from southern Colorado   where
I came from late last night   descending into
the lights of Philadelphia   driving over the
Walt Whitman Bridge to Atlantic City   the diving
horse of Steel Pier long gone   nothing remains
except the pilings and a picture in a display
case in a casino across the boardwalk   once we
spent our summers dancing & diving in pink &
green sequins   The Supremes   The Four Seasons
lovely falsetto voices & our heels kicked up
under the spotlights of the stage   sequins &
fringe sticking to our salt-stained skin
the sea   the surf that pounded our bodies
toes in the sand   sea in our hair   we traipsed
to the dressing rooms   pulled black fishnet
stockings up over our sunburned legs   peeled
ourselves into the elastic strung sequins
fringe swaying like in a breeze   slipped our
feet into hot neon pink tap shoes   a last
brush of our sea-licked hair at the mirror
then lined up by the dusty red velvet curtains
waiting for the intro of our music to begin
arms stretched out to either side   fingers
slightly drooped   head straight ahead   eyes
on the line of velvet on the other side of
stage   when the intro began we'd enter   feet
tapping in unison   slowly turning to the
audience   the kicks low at first then higher

& higher reaching for the spotlights   arms
locked on shoulders   we'd do this twice a
day for 2 weeks each summer   between shows
we'd calypso & cha cha to soul music in the
ballroom over the sea at the end of the pier
watch the woman's thighs clinging to the sides
of the diving horse as they plunged into a
tank of water   peer at the fish swimming by
the portholes of the diving bell   have our
handwriting analyzed by the Univac computer
with alternating blinking lights like the ones
in our dressing room   our portraits painted
by the caricaturists   all this done over the
sea on Steel Pier in Atlantic City   but now
they're country western dancing in a club off
Wildwood & I'm listening to songs of the life
I moved to at 18   away from the sea   the sequins
of nights under the spotlights of a mist-filled
stage   they are wearing boots & black Stetson
hats & singing of a life they dream of   that
I dreamed of   that I wandered to at 18   the
adventure of it in my legs under black fishnet
stockings kicked up to the lights of a sea-
dusted stage

The Miss America Parade

Barbara Helfgott Hyett

Forty-eight white convertibles, a convoy of Queens;
Miss Alabama with a talent for twirling fire;
Miss Delaware plays flute to Peer Gynt's suite;
perched on the rear seat ledge, gown spread
as if she were a tea cozy, Miss Mississippi sings.
Miss Nevada, who rides the whole way standing,
wears a real mink coat.

I learned to twirl when I was nine, play
vibraphone, love pink organza and tulle.
I shoo away the brat squatting for free
at my feet and lick my cotton candy, slowly,
and never blink. First time I've had the quarter
for a beach chair, first row, on the boardwalk.

Washington waves to me. She's gorgeous
but yellow sequins spell her doom. I smile
consolingly. Wyoming's pageboy frizzles.
She lurches as her driver stops short
to hand out Grand Teton National Park balloons.
Now, in full regalia, the Mummers of Philadelphia:
banjos, rhinestones, feathers of some enormous bird,
Oh Dem Golden Slippers stirring the humidity.

I can dance with abandon, like Ginger Rogers,
and sing, with all the necessary gestures,
"Oklahoma." Eleanor Roosevelt
is the woman I most admire.
I believe in God.

The third drum and bugle corps blares by.
A rolling cardboard gingerbread house,
and someone in a baker's hat tosses
Fralinger's saltwater taffy onto my lap.
Lifeguards in real boats row by
on motorized waves. I close my eyes —

I am layered in blue:
long white buttoned gloves, the official scepter,
a velvet runway on the flat back of a float.
Carrying two dozen roses donated
by the New Jersey Jaycees, I manage a tear.
Tidal applause. I wave.

Taste

Rochelle Ratner

Ingredients thrown together
with nothing in common:

I want to scream
to the baker in the window
that his cakes cannot succeed
because too many people watch him.

He smiles and stirs.
He pours the mixture gently.
It took him thirty years
to learn to do that.

Slower than him,
I've spent my life relating.
Always through a showcase window
on Atlantic City's boardwalk
where the man who makes taffy
tries to stretch his life out.

I've been going away
for four years
and coming back once a summer
on vacation —

all the different flavors,
shapes, and colors.
Let me get the candy off my fingers.

Mr. Peanut and a visitor, Susan Subtle, on the Atlantic City Boardwalk.
Photograph © Bud Lee.

Atlantic City Boardwalk:
The Third Attraction
Rochelle Ratner

Searching for the man
at Planter's Peanuts
who, when they were kids,
shook hands with them

his costume
like a straw balloon
around his torso.

This new man
isn't the same:

not tall enough,
and look how that skinny suit
fits him.
Even his jet black arm
shoots out too quickly:
a boat caught in the marsh,
its oars for rudders.

Peanut shells
tossed into water
drift off slowly, floating.

Splendor

Peter E. Murphy

In the gift shops of casinos they sell pens and paper
weights crammed with the slaw of shredded currency,
dim green flakes of thousands of dollars of over tendered bills
crammed into the finger-like cylinders you can take home
to a neighbor or loved one and say, Look what I bought you
at Caesars, and your friend or loved one who lives down the street
or maybe in the other twin bed will protest thanks, grateful
to be thought of on your twelve hour vacation, say it's nice!
and ask about the bus, if it's one of those new double deckers,
if it had a movie that was any good, but what you want to remember
is not the cash green trinket, nor The Color of Money
which you couldn't pay enough attention to to follow on the Parkway,
nor the flamboyant casino whose neon loftiness made you feel
as depressed as hell and whose slot dingdingdings reminded you
of school where you hated the nuns who gave you the hand bell
to ring after lunch, the boys teasing you, calling you Brown
Nose, not knowing the etymology of the phrase, how it got that way,
where it had to go to get brown.

No, you want to talk of splendors like the sea, when you saw it from
the rain-forested boardwalk after losing your quarters and feeding
at the buffet, when you walked down to the beach, stepping on the backs
of a million dead clams still stinking from the winter storm the month
before, how gray could be so beautiful, how if you weren't careful,
you could just walk right into the alluring current and imagine
what lies in that horizon you never knew was there, where the gray
from sky and the gray from the sea kiss their seamless kiss
and you feel like a tongue that wants to enter both mouths
which are really one mouth, all the broth of the subtle
which you were too hungry to notice, all the tears in the flesh
and how the life bubbles up for no reason, how the swell of air
that is so fresh, so alive makes you feel new on this island
at the edge of the continent, that looking over the Atlantic, you can see
your Europe, your Asia, your schizoid Middle East, even your Africa,
all this crashing at your feet in deep rich foam, in gray, in gray.

Atlantic City

Stephen Dunn

To stare at the ocean in winter
   is to know
      the variety in repetition.

It's to understand repetition's secret
   link with solace.
      How often I went to it, lonely,

wanting its sexual music, its applause.
   How often it took my mood
      and deepened it, instructed me

loneliness is nothing special,
   that I was anybody, a man.
      Yesterday at the blackjack table,

a few hundred yards from the shore,
   I doubled-down with eleven
      and drew a three. That was it.

I walked up North Carolina to Arctic
   all alone. The wind suggested
      wonderful movement at sea.

I didn't care. I didn't care if
   the waves were high and white
      or if the seagulls

were dropping clam shells from the sky.
   I had a loser's thought: how wise I was
      for not paying to park.

That's what I said to myself
   far away from myself
      with the ocean now two blocks away;

how wise I was. The houses started to speak
of ruin. Boards on some windows.
Wine bottles in doorways.

To stare at a city half in ruin,
half in glitter,
is to know why the beach

and its beautiful desolation in winter
is a fearsome place
if one comes to it hopeful.

Please, Mister, a man said. In my car,
hidden under the seat,
a quarter for the toll booth.

Atlantic City casino. Photograph © Ray Fisk.

Cocktail Waitress: Atlantic City

Stephen Dunn

Every man I meet wears gold chains,
flashes big bills at the tables,

gives me a fake address, an alias.
Years ago I could take a few Quaaludes

and kill the loneliness with sex,
but now as soon as they speak

I want to be home alone.
I'm getting old. It's gotten so

if I believe anything a man says
I give him three points. If he doesn't

say "nigger" within the first hour
of conversation I give him three more.

I'm thinking of going day shift,
would you believe it, Steve?

Different class of guys, maybe.
But I don't know if I could stand

the nights if no one calls.
Days you can shop, walk the streets,

but at night loneliness is different.
On my night off I try to write,

sometimes go so far into myself
I think there's no getting out.

That poem I gave you about the girl
who disappears in her own room,

did you know, Steve, who she was,
that it wasn't creative writing at all?

Last Chance: Atlantic City 3:45 a.m.

Laura Boss

To G. C.

At 4 a.m. they close the casinos
The pit boss says there will
be three more spins on
the roulette wheel before
the casino closes
This is the third hotel
we've stayed at
in six days
All the hotels
have mirrored ceilings in the casinos,
Velux blankets
The cigarette money is gone
He's just brought me downstairs,
telling me he's found a foolproof
way to win at roulette,
takes the last $10, buys two chips
makes me turn away,
until the wheel stops
He has two chips
on the first and last lines
The middle line is empty
The middle line comes in
We watch the Asian woman
make her last bet
We go to the cheapest place to
eat in the hotel
sit at the counter
I've $10 more for gas
We haven't eaten since lunch
He orders scrambled eggs and sausage
I say I don't want anything

— October 13, 1983

One Good Thing About 24-Hour Gambling

Karen Zaborowski

It's not the chandeliers or the faux crystal
but that the bathrooms are always open
even for your 6 AM run when your jogged-
awake body's three miles of intestines
reconsider that coffee that got you going,
and you race into this Taj Mahal of restrooms
right at your feet.
Heavy glass doors open automatically.
A whoosh of conditioned air hits
your sweaty skin, and your sneakers pad a thick,
Persian rug as you wipe your nose on your sleeve.
The room itself is a long hall of marble stalls
and gleaming gold fixtures where women
polish every corner, even now. There's music —
top 40, taped and piped into your stall
in hourless time, somebody's sound machine
beating to your falling water.
And after, at a scallop-shaped sink,
you spot your puffy, stuck together eyes
in a six-way mirror, your hair,
flat on one side. Two ladies,
still on last night's clock, slouch
in crushed velvet chairs, cupping
their watery drinks. Sequins reflect
matching accessories, smudged makeup
waiting for someone to spin again.
Outside, white waves unfold
like tossed back bedding and the sun,
bloodshot eye on the horizon,
blinks like a neon sign left on too long.
You step off the red carpet onto the boardwalk,
adjust your shorts, break into a run.
The hum of that building fades
behind you while glitter from the next
dares you to stop just once more to command
your simplest, earthly wish.

Leaving Atlantic City

Peter E. Murphy

Next to me on the train pulling away from this island
she uses her cellular phone to call the Casino
a bastard for treating her losses like profit, for smiling
and politeness when she arrives, then waving her off
to the Amtrak in a stretch limo that snaps back
out of the parking lot with her silk jacket still inside.
She calls out the name of the host who seduced her
to this city, the "good boy, good boy" who offered a suite
and a show, and held her hand into the casino to her own table,
her own dealer whose smile gleamed like dice in the chintzy night.
She floated when the host let go, and her falling chips clattered
across the green felt towards craps, and all her cards were jokers,
and the athletic silver ball bounced in and out of her roulette slot
like an unfaithful lover.

Finally she gives up on the host and calls Security
which is busy, then the concierge who tries to urge her
out of her anger, when the batteries fade and she slaps
the phone like a face and screams at it not to die, not yet,
not with so many losses hanging in the air between here
and the resort she is leaving, that there are too many miles,
that her silk jacket is still missing and so is the host
and security, and O, if only there were a red cap or a porter
or an engineer whose fluids passed all their exams, if only
there were someone who could kiss away the mistakes
of the weekend, who could get this phone to work,
who could reverse this train of luck, who could swallow
her scream, someone, a sure thing, she could bet on
in this emergency.

Atlantic City Bus Terminal. Photograph © Donna Connor.

August Memories

Rochelle Ratner

Cougar, Falcon, Lynx,
Impala, Jaguar, Rabbit —
all the sleek, smooth animals
race against the dice
from Atlantic City casinos
to the race track
out by Cardiff Circle
on the Black Horse Pike

And two miles north
there's the parallel road,
the White Horse Pike.
No one remembers
the buggies that long ago
gave them these names,
horses are way too slow
to label cars as,
even race horses.

I remember the motel
I worked at the summer
I learned to drive
where the bartender
took bets on the side.
Classy Kathy
that horse was named,
the only one I bet on
who ever won.

He paid me maybe half
the money, claimed
he didn't have change
and I fell for it.
Black Horse Pike, White
Horse Pike, Stairway to Heaven,
I didn't care what road it was
led out of there.

Progress Report: Atlantic City

Peter E. Murphy

One of my students rushes into my room at the Open House
to see if his parents had been there. No, I say, and he yells,
Damn it! They told me they were coming.
What startles me is his voice. For two months he sits
there quietly failing. I hadn't noticed that I'd never heard
him speak till then, till he ran in to check on his folks
who told him they were going to school to see
how he was doing. What gets me is not that he's here
on parent night, but that he knew his wouldn't show up.
He says they like the casinos. This has happened before.
In this latitude where even hurricanes become disorganized
before slamming into shore, there is no barrier to retard
the unnatural disasters spun into motion. The odds plunge
like high school students dropping out of class, like chips
falling between cracks in the boardwalk where a family squats
in the summer, having rented their home to tourists who've come
to game. They live under wood through Labor Day, then emerge
to cheer the Miss America photo-op down the runway.
And one morning on the beach, a contestant tosses a Frisbee
through the foam, blinds the camera with her beautiful, capped teeth,
finds the corpse of a drifter under a lifeguard boat.

Atlantic City
Shilpi Niyogi

Springsteen, yes, native
Jersey son
But Louis Malle
with visions of lemons
erasing the stench
of salt-water fish
of charred brick and rotting windowpanes
in the hot cracked asphalt
carcass of a city

no parasols on the Boardwalk
no summer holiday
no trump cards left
just waves crashing
and neon flashing as arthritic hands
pull the handle in hopes
of buying Park Place

my father drives down the shore
everyday through Berlin and Hammonton
to blueprints and a drawing board
new high school coming up in the marshes

no garish monuments
no ballrooms
no baccarat
just classrooms
for the native sons
and daughters

Elephant Hotel

Barbara Helfgott Hyett

On a narrow slip of sand where the boardwalk
and the spine of the city finally let up,
a ninety-two-ton wooden elephant
faces the sea. She stands on hollow legs,
marking the tideline with her old toes, every joint,
Victoriana, still crimped and watertight.

She has survived the whim of her creator,
vacuity, a waterfront hotel
as high as the Sphinx. She is the one
sight to see on the honky-tonk frontier.
Her hide is painted, sheathed in tin,
a single shade of gray.

A Quaker condemned her to South Jersey,
the salt-marsh jungle of bayberry and pine.
A real-estate investor promoted her for the crowd.
The Pennsylvania Railroad was laid at her feet.
Steamboats chugged in from Somers Point; stagecoach
connections, mule-drawn trolleys from town.

And they came, pleasure seekers, across the dunes
to sign her guest book and gape.
A stairway spiraled them into her
from the rear, her innards
timbered, partitioned into floors,
eleven rooms with a vaulted hall.

Lovers slept in the summer cottage of her flanks.
Under ruffles and parasols, ladies in corsets
considered the consequences of immensity, then
climbed inside her to look out the window of her eye.
They sipped tea in the ornate howdah on her back
and took the tonic of iodine air.

Ocean continues to tease her thick ankles,
spuming foam as white as her unconvincing tusks.
Her trunk hangs limp, noseholes buried in a bucket
not big enough. Sunrise glazes her glass eye
and variegates the pigeons roosting in her ear.
On the rim of the tide, poker-faced, she listens.

Lucy, the Margate Elephant. Photograph © Walter Choroszewski.

Lucy the Elephant

Mark O'Hara

As a child I toured
her creaking innards: I remember
tiny staircases, the caretaker's bathroom.
My parents had to coax me from her belly.
In my head she stood with other
campy structures we passed
driving to the shore:
the restaurant shaped like a ship,
the three-story figures that guarded
gas stations, farm markets
and frozen custard stands.

It seemed each time I forgot her
Lucy resurfaced. Far from abandoned,
she wore a new skin against the salt air.
Mr. Rogers showed my kids
her metal plates and the shiny colors
of her paint. She appeared
in an AP photo, headed
for another national registry.
It occurred to me, oddly,
that I must see her again —
I was like a trainer who missed
her shambling and wry jokes.

Next vacation we'll leave the Midwest
for my parents'.
A day trip to Margate,
and luck will have it that
my children can tour Lucy's rebuilt body.
Looking out the portal of her eye
they'll command her to break
her moorings, their importunate voices
causing her to shatter the chains
of her foundation, her thunderous

trumpet sounding through every casino
in Atlantic City and clear
to the lighthouse
as she carries them ponderously
across the beach for a swim
in the smooth green waters.

The Drowning

Eileen Spinelli

When I was four
A carload of relatives
Drove to Margate
In an old Dodge
Windows down —
No air-conditioning then
Till we came to
The wooden elephant
By the sea.

And the men carried
Baskets of cold chicken
Mason jars of tea
And the women
Spread patched blankets
On the sand.

A distant
Twelve year old cousin
I'd never seen
Till that morning
Came over, smiling
Dripping
Wanting to play big sister
Wanting to take me
Into the surf.

My mother said
No,
Distracting me with
Red tin pail and shovel.
We dug shallow holes
To china
As my cousin ran zig-zagging
Away.

Afternoon moved
Slowgolden as the sun
My cousin's mother
Began to call her:
Lottie!
A green bi-plane
Engined past
Trailing a streamer
Freemont's Fudge.

Lottie!
Louder
Across the bright beach
The rocks
In time across the water
And the shadows.

After dark
The men bought
Oyster sandwiches.
You have to eat
They told the women
Who shivered in sweaters
Whose lips tasted of salt.

At midnight
Carlights
Flashlights
Long replacing the sun
Beamed seaward
Catching a crumpled towel
A bucket of shells
An ice cream wrapper.
Nothing more.

The men
Took turns
Driving home.

The women huddled
In the back seat
Where Lottie's blue dress
(She would have worn it
After swimming)
Flapped
Against their knees.

Beached Whales off Margate

Stephen Dunn

One day they just started rolling up,
six pilot whales from way out.
Two hundred people pushed three of them back, oh
it took hours. I tell you all this
because two hundred people usually hurt
what they touch. But not this time.
After it was done, they all stood around
for a while, like the humans they used to be,
lamenting the three who were dead.
Separateness set in slowly; an aerial shot
would have shown a group moving away
from its center, leaving in ones and twos
toward their large, inconsiderate houses.

Somers Point

A. R. Ammons

What are you doing out here
this windy on the headland
said the bay reeds bent inland,

their bounding tassels like
blurred drops trying to rain ashore,
the bay water thrashing

to land or get away to the open,
the holly, its held leaves
jangling tambourines, the

whipping cypresses simmering and
seething:
oh I said I've come out here

to hide in the trembling
from my trembling, storm roars
outsounding blood roars, sprints

of pulse surpassed by clacking leaves,
to count how many, many
particulars ease could come into.

Ocean City

A. R. Ammons

Island-end here is
elongated as a
porpoise's nose, all
lawns and houses
except one spot
where bending property lines have
turned out odd,
giving this plot
the sanctuary of contention —
bayberry, wild
cherry, plum thicket:
a shore hawk
knows the spot,
knows grackles, sparrows,
cardinals, even
mockingbirds cluster here:
he drops by &
right here in town
some early mornings wilderness
meets wilderness
in a perfect stare.

Autumnal Holiday

Virginia Masland Stetser

Ocean City, NJ

One year it was the geese.
All chose one day to fly south,
arrows piercing clouds
or mathematic symbols meaning
greater than any country's holiday.

Another year it was swallows
lining roofs and wires that dove
all at once to ravish bayberries
in one brief hour. Come and gone,
as branches clenched their fists
and shook beneath the onslaught.

This year monarch butterflies.
Oh, a few straggled by before,
some after, but it was one day
only that they came and kept on
coming, in epidemic flitters,
as though there'd never be another
wind-hushed time to travel.

They pass on different days,
geese, birds, butterflies,
and some years not at all,
but those are rare.

Ocean City Music Pier. Photograph © Joseph Paduano.

Walkabout/Ocean City

Walter Bargen

It's a good sign that these hard-shelled
insects with their stubborn raspings are here;

but almost no one can hear them in their few
square feet of splotched sand, between foot-long

hot dogs and the high dreamy fluff of cotton
candy; there declaring an uneasy allegiance

with the shadowy silences under miles of boarded
walk fronting surf and jewelry shops, over-priced

shells and fortune tellers, sometimes three
to a tent with tarot, crystal, and palm readings;

and still there's a slow winding line to the future,
as gulls on guardrails, or flying overhead,

voice their impatient schedules to the perpetually
moving crowds, out to measure themselves

against another evening; enthralled legions
quickly close ranks as a few strollers fall away

early, weak of heart or simply tired, seeing
the rounded, rotting stumps of wharf pilings

that step off into the sea, each one shorter
than the last until only a turbulent ghostly

foam marks a vanishing, where others once
walked arm-in-arm, tailored and parasoled,

unhurried and leaning on what's not now there,
whispering vows only the sea keeps, but after

the tide pushes closer that bitten wafer of moon,
its gleaming sickle sweeping low, as if harvesting

waves, the children draw back with their skate-
boards and shouts, to temporary homes surrounded

by smooth pebbled lawns, places where they don't
grow old fast enough, and later will always be

caught remembering, where the old linger
on benches back against a painting of pastel

evenings, listening to the echoes of footfalls
among crickets.

Watching Them Ride the Rides

Karen Zaborowski

Ocean City boardwalk

They spin and whirl in giant teacups,
hair straight out, foreheads pressed back,
teeth, gums shining.
I wave at every rotation and know
this is the moment mothers need,
the time when children are happy.
No expressions to decipher,
no drama to diagnose,
no young pain,
only the joy of getting spun,
enthralled for a time,
and I exhale and believe
I am doing my job.
I am keeping that promise of the heart,
the one I never realized I was making,
and here they come spinning by again,
waving, making sure I see.

Disruption

Therése Halscheid

Ocean City, NJ

By midnight, the water had risen
all around the sea houses

submerged
the wood docks, splashed over

the bottom decks
hiding white lawns with smooth stones

and shell gardens,

hiding the fear of those of us
who stayed, trapped

by waves breaking
beneath the flickering lamps —

it was too late

to push the wet car over
the sopping bridge, it was too late

to save the finned ones tossed
from the sea

slapping their gills
against the exhausted earth

when the tide pulled back,
and the small town rose crying

to wring itself out
as everything stilled.

Corsons Inlet

A. R. Ammons

I went for a walk over the dunes again this morning
to the sea,
then turned right along
   the surf
                rounded a naked headland
                and returned
   along the inlet shore:

it was muggy sunny, the wind from the sea steady and high,
crisp in the running sand,
     some breakthroughs of sun
  but after a bit

continuous overcast:

the walk liberating, I was released from forms,
from the perpendiculars,
     straight lines, blocks, boxes, binds
of thought
into the hues, shadings, rises, flowing bends and blends
        of sight:

               I allow myself eddies of meaning:
yield to a direction of significance
running
like a stream through the geography of my work:
  you can find
in my sayings
            swerves of action
            like the inlet's cutting edge:
         there are dunes of motion,
organizations of grass, white sandy paths of remembrance
in the overall wandering of mirroring mind:

but Overall is beyond me: is the sum of these events
I cannot draw, the ledger I cannot keep, the accounting
beyond the account:

in nature there are few sharp lines: there are areas of
primrose
    more or less dispersed;
disorderly orders of bayberry; between the rows

of dunes,
irregular swamps of reeds,
though not reeds alone, but grass, bayberry, yarrow, all . . .
predominantly reeds:

I have reached no conclusions, have erected no boundaries,
shutting out and shutting in, separating inside
    from outside: I have
    drawn no lines:
    as

manifold events of sand
change the dune's shape that will not be the same shape
tomorrow,

so I am willing to go along, to accept
the becoming
thought, to stake off no beginnings or ends, establish
    no walls:

by transitions the land falls from grassy dunes to creek
to undercreek: but there are no lines, though
    change in that transition is clear
    as any sharpness: but "sharpness" spread out,
allowed to occur over a wider range
than mental lines can keep:

the moon was full last night: today, low tide was low:
black shoals of mussels exposed to the risk
of air
and, earlier, of sun,

waved in and out with the waterline, waterline inexact,
caught always in the event of change:
     a young mottled gull stood free on the shoals
     and ate
to vomiting: another gull, squawking possession, cracked a crab,
picked out the entrails, swallowed the soft-shelled legs, a ruddy
turnstone running in to snatch leftover bits:

risk is full: every living thing in
siege: the demand is life, to keep life: the small
white blacklegged egret, how beautiful, quietly stalks and spears
     the shallows, darts to shore
          to stab — what? I couldn't
    see against the black mudflats — a frightened
    fiddler crab?

      the news to my left over the dunes and
reeds and bayberry clumps was
     fall: thousands of tree swallows
     gathering for flight:
     an order held
     in constant change: a congregation
rich with entropy: nevertheless, separable, noticeable
    as one event,
         not chaos: preparations for
flight from winter,
cheet, cheet, cheet, cheet, wings rifling the green clumps,
beaks
at the bayberries
  a perception full of wind, flight, curve,
  sound:
  the possibility of rule as the sum of rulelessness:
the "field" of action
with moving, incalculable center:

in the smaller view, order tight with shape:
blue tiny flowers on a leafless weed: carapace of crab:

snail shell:
>>pulsations of order
>>in the bellies of minnows: orders swallowed,
broken down, transferred through membranes
to strengthen larger orders: but in the large view, no
lines or changeless shapes: the working in and out, together
and against, of millions of events: this,
>>>so that I make
>>>no form
>>>formlessness:

orders as summaries, as outcomes of actions override
or in some way result, not predictably (seeing me gain
the top of a dune,

the swallows
could take flight — some other fields of bayberry
>>could enter fall
>>berryless) and there is serenity:

>>no arranged terror: no forcing of image, plan,
or thought:
no propaganda, no humbling of reality to precept:

terror pervades but is not arranged, all possibilities
of escape open: no route shut, except in
>the sudden loss of all routes:

>>I see narrow orders, limited tightness, but will
not run to that easy victory:
>>still around the looser, wider forces work:
>>I will try
>to fasten into order enlarging grasps of disorder, widening
scope, but enjoying the freedom that
Scope eludes my grasp, that there is no finality of vision,
that I have perceived nothing completely,
>>that tomorrow a new walk is a new walk.

Beach walk. Photograph © Ray Fisk.

How Not Much Has Changed

Kyle Laws

I traveled from Stone Harbor to Avalon
to Sea Isle City to Strathmere to Ocean City
on the roads of the back bays from bridge
to bridge   houses & fishing shacks facing
the sea   piers stretched over the marsh
grasses   boats for hire   fishing poles
crab nets   I wanted to ride the edge of
my life   the edge of the beginning
barrier reefs that protected me where
no matter the storm   the wind I was
enveloped in   the arms of these back
bays held me & held the canopies of
tall oaks   cedar forests that became the
Victorians of Cape May   grey weathered
cedar shakes of small salt boxes   tall
masted ships pulled into harbor   squat
commercial fishing boats   the floats
of nets piled on the docks like stacks
of tropical fruits: oranges grapefruits
huge lemons & limes   the first impression
is one of a cargo carried from afar
brought to these islands of Wildwood &
Anglesea   thought dangerous   too vulnerable
only good for grazing cattle on the grasses
of the dunes   once the grasses were almost
gone   overgrazed   overtread by people on
the way to the sea   and a piano plays on
on South Street in Philadelphia   trickling
down to the river that empties into the bay
into the sea at Diamond Beach   into the torn
hull of a concrete ship that strayed from its
mooring   got stuck in sand   settled in so
quickly & there it has laid for 80 years
splitting open a little more each year   how
things stay the same like the Villas 5 & 10:

penny candy in the same place only smaller
hair ribbons down the same dark row   Gracie
at the soda fountain now closed since Clem
died but the same flavors still up on the
Sealtest board: vanilla strawberry peach
Clem fixing cherry cokes after school
Cora's asking if I remember this person &
that & Gracie says after I continue to reply
no that I always was such a good kid   never
got into trouble   didn't mix much   was a
loner & I think of this as I walk the length
of the town in the sand by the bay   how I
laughed when Gracie said that   replied that
I still am the same   how not much has changed
how I am like this village on the bay

Thinking of Love at the Jersey Shore

Norma Voorhees Sheard

On the way to Cape May, we stopped
to walk along the winter sands
of Avalon, shoulder touching shoulder,
our steps barely marking the hard beach.
The sea, of course, had lured us,
a welter of gray sinews
fanning foam and debris on shore.
Which of us spotted them first —
the chanks and whelks scattered like
rune bones farther than we could see.
We darted like children among them,
reluctant to leave any, our pockets
bulging, the crooks of our arms ladened.
We could not have it all.

Finally, we had to scan each iridescent
whorl for the slightest crack or bubble,
gathering, discarding till we knew
our fingers again — swollen red,
aching with grit and salt.

Savings

Warren Woessner

Sea Isle City, NJ

Pop wouldn't touch the junk-shop souvenirs
but lined the dash with free samples
from where we went to fish:
a driftwood fork, chunks
of fossil coral, gray basalt
foamed with twisted holes.
I keep them in a drawer
with clip-on shades,
a Barlow knife, a lure.

Out looking for birds,
I walk the shore eyes down,
pass by limpets, glass shards,
skate eggs and tangled line.
Low sun glows through a scallop shell —
the hinge still flexes,
a scrap of meat sticks
where the muscle was.
I stop. The first charm
picks me out.

Bird Cursing

Gerald Stern

For King Hohan Topatrapanning

I want to watch my sweet body go out again into the beach plums
and hang again with all that luxury
between the marsh islands of Stone Harbor
and the monkey gardens of Anglesea.

I want to see my dark shoulders rise and fall
in oblique reference to the cry of hunger
and the large shadow slipping over the lawns.

I want to hear the great grasses hiss with delight
as Wildwood drops back again into the sand.

Jersey Girl
Helen Ruggieri

Wildwood, NJ

I want to sing by the ocean and
sleep by the sea.
I want to swim,
to be buoyed up,
to flutter kick and breast stroke,
I want grit under my toes
sun on my shoulders.
I want destiny to find me
and give out my address.

I want pizza and coke
a plane waving me where to go
and everywhere I look
slick oily bodies
competing for attention.

I want to dance in a glass room
with someone who lives to move,
all sultry and salt.
I want to scan the boardwalk
for every opportunity.

I want that pulse in me
a shell for my heart
calling the mambo,
the cha cha cha,
everything cherry pink
and apple blossom white.

Wildwood boardwalk. Photograph © Joseph Paduano.

On What the Future of Civilization Depends

Bruce Curley

I

"YO! Youse guys know where the party is tonight?"
The third of the summer blondes
Asks the streetcornered muscled boys.

"Right here, baby! Get outta dat car
And come over here!
We'll show youse how ta party!"
Smiles Tenderness Tony to his friends
First, and then to the summer blondes,
Fully aware of what hangs in the balance.

"Well, we're kinda lookin' for real men.
Youse guys don't look old enough
Ta drive our cars or even work on our engines!
Wheel it Marie!" laughs Angela.

They cruise around the Wildwood block,
Circle and return, compelled by a mating ceremony
As old as any migrating naked rhizopod's
As insistent as any remoras on a tiger shark
As powerful as any copulating American saddle horses.

At the same time Tenderness Tony and Angela circle each other warily,
Hundreds of thousands of others dance the same dance floor
To repeat ancient and glorious tribal mating rites
Less understood than the circling rites of shark whales off Tahiti.

II

I know many who do not see the wonder of this.
Instead, they spend their days saying to whoever will listen,
"See! See there! This life is only abuse, death, destruction,
Hate and finally pain, pain, pain and cruelty!"
And it is not just journalists saying this these days.

Perhaps such as these have never visited Wildwood, NJ
At the height of the mating season.
For there, on any given sultry summer night
When the air is as thick with mating phrenomes
As the Brazilian rain forest, everything is possible.

"Youse guys still where the party is tonight?"
Now it is Marie talking, newly revealed as the princess in waiting
Who throws out the challenge to all willing to chance the future.
All three boys respond by raising themselves high
To preen their feathered haircuts like cocks
About to meet their flaring hens.

"Yeah, Baby! I'm here for youse only tonight!
He's 'VAA VAA VOOOMM' Vic! I'm Tenderness Tony.
Dis here's happiness itself,
Whose otherwise known as Loverboy Louie."

This night laden with romance and possibility,
Despite the miles of backed up traffic
Tens of thousands in cars, clubs, bars,
All along these dazzling street-lit courting avenues
Rhythmically step to this genetically programmed dance
Unbothered by anything but the moment of contact.

Like a novice nun tenderly fingering her rosary,
Theresa brushes her hair with tender strokes
As Marie parks the car in one swift motion.
All three watch the boys in the car mirror,
Well aware of what their charged rituals
Are producing in the awaiting Tony, Vic, and Louie.
Each reapplies her love-red glossy candy flavored lipstick,
Sprays wave after wave of perfume on her neck and breasts
And saunters over to her instant date for that night.

III

For those who snootily laugh at these young people,
Who dismiss their substandard english or their different ways,
I ask youse to please consider the following.

It is on the perpetual success of such everyday rituals
Far more than on what laws Congress passes,
Or breakthroughs our medical schools make,
Or discount rate the Fed establishes,
Or new worlds the Hubble discovers,
Or programs the President proposes,
That the future of civilization depends.

"Youse guys ready to party?" shouts Marie.
"Yooooooooo!!! Honey! The party's just begun!"
Answers Tenderness Tony. "The party's just begun!"

Seventeen years later,
Within a mile of where her parents met,
The oldest of Tony and Marie's girls
Drives by some guys on the corner of 58th and Atlantic
In "Wildwood by the Sea,"
And shouts, "YO! Youse guys know where the party is tonight?"
When she does, on the successful answer to her question,
Will the future of civilization depend.

In the Dunes

Kyle Laws

my grandparents buried north
of Cape May Court House
graves unmarked except for
the small brass wedge
that cuts old beach grass
where cattle used to graze
a plumber & his wife from Phoenixville
a great bird-serpent rising into the night
how the gulls would flock his shoulders
as he ran a knife down the spine
of flounder taken from the bay
gills open to the wind of birds
he had those large hands that could
unthread a pipe laid deep in this sand
that threads our feet, our toes,
salt grass, and the hot breath
of old cattle buried in the dunes
those old skulls of brute jerseys
laid down beside my grandfather
& his bride from Phoenixville

Cape May

Rod Tulloss

At the end of Rising
Sun Tavern Road
honeysuckle grows in
the wild white roses.
And above the harbor at Great Egg
an immense white bird is
breakfasting in river shallows;
green fly marshes stretch
out to the sea haze;
and the road sides are
starred with yellow hawkweed and
morning glory.

This afternoon, we
laid our keys
by a blue glass lamp
in a blue room by the sea.
It was the heat
of the day. We
had to take two showers.

*vi.*10.79
for Mary

Front porch of the Queen Victoria, Cape May, NJ. Photograph © Vincent T. Marchese.

Cape May

Joel Lewis

The cool of pre-rain weather tints the air
& soft breezes jostle shingles on a pink
gingerbread fort on Hughes & Decatur.
The news stays old here on these
latitudes that swing on through Virginia
& so unlike that Jersey we own;
Paterson's stark inattention, Linden's ocean
of refineries & of stoop dwellers
hooting across Hoboken's urban dawn silence. September
here, with the beach people back home
& this "south Cape Isle" returned
to the mix of sadness & intuition
that's a summer town off-season.

The boardwalk arcades empty in morning's
hanging blue & the surf tom-toms
narrow Poverty Beach with each sloppy wave a
bud already to burst. Up Ocean Avenue is
Victorian cold focus — Our guidebook's #2A:
The Seaview House, once the "thumbprint" cottage
of one Evan Morris. From a builder's illustrated
catalog the proper Victorian could keep up
with his neighbors through a mix 'n match
of carved balconies, elaborate spandrels
& rooster-comb Acroterions. Now listen to
the creaking from massed rocking chairs
on the Chalfonte Hotel's veranda, the Summer draining
with each strolling couple.

The gaslight streets of the historic East End
have been carefully restored to the epoch
of imaginary childhood sing-a-longs
'round the Mason & Hamlin. Here, as
adults, we can imagine our dear phantom
Victorian predecessors arriving by Pennsy's Seashore line

for another season of communal dining
& formal conversation. So, enjoy your illusions
& be an envious ghost in this world of genteel
summer pleasures. Simply count the gables
as you stroll along Corgie Street just as the sun
gets sucked under Delaware Bay, leaving only
gaslight to read the half-moon's script.

* * *

Sunset Beach is someone's attempt at art photography.
— A black handbook of waves pounds the breakwater
& as all signs on Sunset Blvd. declare,
"Sunken Ship" remains wrecked offshore
— the Atlantus, a prototype concrete ship built during
the steel shortage of WWI. And within site of this barnacle
motel, my wife of one year & I join a clump
of rainy-day sandhogs for a morning of prospecting
for Cape May Diamonds. Though newspapers may have tried
to sell us moonscapes, here we are — picking
milk-white drops from a crumbling shore.

And, perhaps, there are many kinds of stuff
in the concerns of life &, perhaps, empty effort,
that drama of the non-commodity, is one edge
of the daily connection. But the hailing frequencies
of my mind's lining blend in with
a million disparate possibilities & then only one, you
now against the windows of my eyes as our
forgotten instants return to spiral between us
as we watch the whole Atlantic spread out before us
in order to sleep, at sunset's bell.

At the Cape May Hotel
Peter E. Murphy

Sharing this geriatric swimming pool at night with a fiftieth reunion
of the class of '41, no one slips under water or strays
toward the diving end. I watch from the bloodwarm spa
forbidden to them by pacemakers, the flab white chests that bob
up and down like slow motion dancers to an inner Guy Lombardo
which even they can't hear above the rhythm of the splattering water
and the tape of the post modern lifeguard whose *Beasty Boys*
splashes like a cold rain from hell, cracking the dry ears
that have become brittle from war and work and the mildewed repetition
of retirement. Today on the Autumn tour after strolling
through preserved Victorian houses, they saw where the Atlantic
slaps against the Delaware and studied the remains of a concrete ship,
whose wrecked bow points toward the stars in the distant shallow sky.

One gray mama tows her old man by the armpits toward deep water.
His eyes are closed, his lips barely open, limping for breaths
of steamy air. She turns him over and places her mouth
on his mouth until his eyes open and his face breaks
into lights that float above the crooked wakes of water.
These lovers do not let go, barely stopping for air
as their feet slide from side to side above bottomless suffocation.
Another couple wades out, and then another, until this extremity
is crammed like a dance floor. Old men, old women, suspended
above the boundaries of war, of labor, of houses and homes,
and the grandchildren of grand children. They hover
in the comfortable arms of the water, pressing against familiar lips,
holding for a moment their breath in the depths of limit and dissolution.

Afternoon at Cape May Beach

Michael D. Riley

Always the fatigue-green waves rolling into white spray
            and curdling foam, time sanded down at our feet,
            filled only with mirrorings like wet glass,
            overtreading footprints, half-buried shells,
            the heaving shoulders of the surf unfatigued forever

A knobbed horizon of anonymous fishing boats,
            a harmless Dunkirk of grey vessels on a grey plane,
            sea and sky met grey on grey, graced briefly
            by a white schooner, swan among the paddling tugs,
            pulled effortlessly past our eyes

Kids romp and jig stiff-legged up and down the sand,
            chasing their elbows and knees, laughing and crying
            almost at once, as full of disjointed energy
            as the colonial toy with the segmented wooden man
            who dances on the spanked piece of wood

The loud family well-matched on the next blankets
            squawk like gulls at one another, anger and love
            the same barking tone, a steady fiber
            of tough brown words their staff of life
            (two of their five progeny dig a hole nearby
            big enough to bury both parents in)

Young women pulled along by their full hips
            sway lightly breast to thigh and ankle,
            each of us sculpted for ends beyond these ends,
            carved flesh and bone for others —
            to bear, repair, embrace them, some of us
            to stare and take notes, square the circles
            of our lives together where we find them beached

Small planes lumber just beyond the shore
            trailing commercial messages. I supply my own:

This tide along our bloodstream flows. Each grain
a seed. Together we are distanced here.
Vast anonymous comfort comes. This slow propelling life
observing. My messages incomplete begin. See next plane.

Kites of good memories, bright and precise and small,
    dip and soar above the waves, then drift back lazily
    toward the beach and all of us on holiday beneath them,
    their grounding ropes almost invisible at this distance

Hawk-Watch at Cape May

John Pember

Without spotting scope or bird book
I felt as if I were crashing
some stranger's party.
With all eyes to the sky,
necks stretched back
just short of snapping,
the birders never noticed.

Ten o'clock south,
someone shouted,
a pair!
I've got them!
Me, too!
from two other watchers
with binoculars pressed
firmly to their faces.
And the crowd on the platform
built above the marsh
turned to the south
and saw dark dots, no more,
against the leaden October sky.
Cooper's hawks said the ranger
and marked them on the tally board.
One of the pros
with a monocular on a tripod
had already turned away
and was the first to announce,
One at two o'clock east!
A peregrine, I think.
And the crowd turned again,
seeing nothing, really,
and waited for the ranger to confirm,
while the pros were already swiveling,
each trying to be the first
to call out and make the crowd shift.

Condors from the south!
I wanted to cry out,
not content with spectator sports.
Auks from the east!
Penguins at six o'clock!
Hummingbirds everywhere!
But I didn't —
left it to the pros
with the anxious faces
and their crowd
with no faces at all.

Cape May Point

Warren Woessner

Snapshots of sun
silhouette scoters
close to shore.
We duck buckshot sand
pick off an eider
with the scope.
Farther out, gannets
wheel and dive,
show fish how to fly.
We watch the sea-spears
at 30 power, wind,
birds, waves blowing
straight in our eyes.

Notes from Cape May Point

Tom Plante

Bikers and bathers
are on the move.
August is ending.

Raptors search for lunch
above the marsh,
gathering strength for
the flight to Delaware.

Monarchs flap from
fence to flower.

Time passes in its fashion,
tides and dunes in flux.
Migrations are counted on
like an old reliable watch
though it sometimes
slows or stops.

A bumble bee finds
another blue flower.
A monarch follows.
Another bee, another bush.

Herring gulls and black backs
battle the breeze.

Decisions crowd my sandals.
A swim before it rains?
Or follow a birder's advice:
smear pine cones with
peanut butter. Hang them.
Sit back and watch.

Cape May Lighthouse. Photograph © Joseph Paduano.

199 *Steps to the Top of the Lighthouse*

Kyle Laws

I stood at the bottom of the circular
staircase   there are 199 steps to the
top   six landings in between where you
can look out on the sea   the estuary now
a bird sanctuary   the circular streets
of town all leading to the sea   this you
can see from the landings   windows cut
into layers of brick growing thinner &
thinner as you rise up into the grey sky
all is thick at the bottom   thick & round-
bellied   a woman sits in a corner in the
dark   tells you that you can make it to the
top if you take advantage of the landings
both railings had been added to make the
ascent easier   each landing tells a story
what has been taken/washed away by the sea:
buildings   silos   an older lighthouse
on this landing   this extension   this
intrusion into the sea   the town built
over an estuary   pilings above the water
that rise & fall   sidewalks of wood planks
over the sand   reeds & grass creeping
through   speculators who sold two-storied
dreams   scattered on the circular streets
are bits & pieces of the old places   the
second story of a grand white house became
a bar off Diamond Beach   I remember eating
there in 1964   Barbra Streisand on the
jukebox   the inside was dark & small &
felt as if the sea had rushed through
it was damp & smelled of salt   the sea
had rushed through many places in the
1962 March storm   we watched from
the kitchen door of our house on the
bluff as one piling after another of

the bulkhead was taken with each wave
the bay would smash hard against what
remained & as it retreated   drew in its
breath   it would take another piling with
it   draw the yielding blackened wood into
its arms & roll back into its turbulent
bed   it was like my father who took all
things to bed with him   wrapped them up
in his arms & swept them away   at times
we shook our heads because we did not
understand how it was done   but he was
like the bay we lived on   this is all
at the bottom of the landing   there are
199 steps to the top   at each landing
I am told a story   this was once a
religious community   the Presbyterians
owned it as a retreat   St. Mary's by
the Sea was a hotel   the town radiated
from the meeting place on the circle in
the center   I see red roofs from the
landings   exotic birds fly into the
sanctuary   my father's parents were
both ministers   they have retreated to
the sea   speculators are building homes
south of town   the sidewalks are of wood
the sea rushes under them when the moon is
full   when the wind blows   when the light
wavers from the top of the lighthouse
only 100 more steps to go   a trolley ran
on rails from the bottom of the steps to
Cape May   it ran the street by the sea
you could go to town on a Saturday night
eat steamed clams & mussels   drink beer
at the Ugly Mug   bring home salt water
taffy   but it was the ride on the rails

the sea in your hair   the salt from an
afternoon swim still on your skin   the
waves against your body   the tumult   the
caress   the embrace   that stayed with you
letting go & letting the sea take you to
its bed   leaving you on the edge of foam
of tide   when it was done   that is what
you take with you to town   on the rail
the glide on sun bleached sand   when you
sit in the corner of a bar   it is in the
clams   the broth that tastes of sea   they
slide down rough   they have the tumult in
them   there are 49 steps to go   this could
be any place   this circle of stairs   but
as soon as I say it   I know it is not true
I have been from state to state & nowhere
feels quite like this   nowhere is there
quite the tumult   the tumble   it will stay
with me   rise on the wings of a grey &
white gull   follow the boats through the
canal   break the protection of the jetties
Higbee's Beach is not far   where Father
would go to watch the women swim nude
he would stand in the reeds & tall grass
after finishing up at the Gulf Station at
the end of Pennsylvania Avenue   wash his
hands in the stained sink   drive the
Plymouth over the draw bridge to the end
of the road across the canal   watch women
in the flow of the moon   tide rushing
their bodies   letting go to the arms of
the sea   there is a railing at the top of
the lighthouse   you can walk outside the
light   the sea for all its tumult is not
this unsteady   but it was here I was

reaching for   when I climb back down I
will run for the sea   eager for its lick
of my legs   its tumult   I will wait for
dark   look up from the sand of Higbee's
Beach   the moon on my skin   to the beam
from the top of the lighthouse as it
circles the sea

With the Nuns at Cape May Point

David Earle Anderson

For Kristin

Yesterday a shark was reported cruising
  just beyond the jetty and so tonight
  I scan the distance, watching and waiting
For my child, to learn she is alive.
  Tonight only the black line of a ferry,
  shapeless in the distance, bears on.
Given shore and ocean, at evening
  there is no climate, the bay
  dissolving in the butter of the setting sun.
A procession of nuns, on vacation or retreat,
  approach the receding tide, carol
  the water. We felt their voices advancing;
The vacationers fell back, dumb. Both ways
  the form is older than any of us,
  each coming and going clumsy.
The tide returns, running over sleep. My wife
  is a nun, processing; my child a shark, waiting;
  and I, a ship melting in the night.

Contributors

A. R. Ammons is the Goldwin Smith Professor of Poetry at Cornell University. His work has received numerous honors, including a Guggenheim Fellowship, the National Book Critics Circle Award, the Bollingen Prize, the Ruth Lilly Poetry Prize, and a MacArthur Prize Fellow Award. He has won the National Book Award twice: in 1993 for his book *Garbage*, and in 1973 for *Collected Poems 1951-1971*. From 1952 to 1961 he was an executive of a New Jersey firm that manufactured biological and medical glassware.

David Earle Anderson is a journalist and writer in Washington, DC, who has published poems in *The Christian Century*, *Liturgy*, and *Response*; critical essays in *Christianity in Crisis*, *Conscience*, and *Present Tense*; and political writings in *The Progressive*.

Scott Edward Anderson is the author of *Walks in Nature's Empire: Exploring The Nature Conservancy's Preserves in New York State*. Although currently residing in New York's Hudson River Valley, he lived for a number of years in Hoboken, NJ, where he was part of the mid-1980s poetry scene at Maxwell's and Cafe Elysian. He and his wife, who grew up in Montclair, NJ, frequently vacation "down the shore."

Walter Bargen has published his poems in *Spoon River Poetry Review*, *Sycamore Review*, and *Poet & Critic*, among others, and his first published short story appeared in *American Letters and Commentary*. In 1994 he co-edited *Rising Waters: Reflections on the Years of the Great Flood*, an anthology of twenty-seven mostly midwestern writers. His fourth book of poems, *The Vertical River*, was published in 1995 by Timberline Press.

Judi K. Beach has poetry in *Tar River Poetry*, *Cape Rock*, *Without Halos*, *Writer's Digest*, and *Earth's Daughters*, among others, and has been anthologized in *Life on the Line: Selections on Words and Healing* and *What's Become of Eden: Poems of Family at the End of the Century*. She has also written a textbook, *Developing a Writer's Eye . . . and Ear, Nose, Tongue, and Skin*.

Jeanne Marie Beaumont grew up in the suburbs of Philadelphia and spent summers "down the shore." Her poems have appeared in many national magazines, including *The Nation*, *Harper's*, and *Poetry*, and in the anthologies *Mondo Barbie* and *Mondo Marilyn*.

Claire C. Beskind says she began writing poetry in 1975, finding it offered "therapeutic distance" following a painful time during which she suffered a stroke that incapacitated her left hand. She is a member of Delaware Valley Poets, Inc., and works as an evaluator for a psychological testing company.

Mary C. Bilderback lives on Long Beach Island and is a member of the Biology Department of Georgian Court College in Lakewood, NJ. She has had poems published in *Without Halos*, *The SandPaper*, and *The Beachcomber*.

Laura Boss is the founder and editor of LIPS, a poetry journal based in Montclair, NJ. Her awards for poetry include first prize in the Poetry Society of America's Gordon Barber Poetry Contest; an American Literary Translators Association (ALTA) Award; and fellowships in poetry from the New Jersey State Council on the Arts. Her books of poetry include *Stripping* (Chantry Press, 1982) and the ALTA Award-winning *On the Edge of the Hudson* (Cross-Cultural Communications, 1986).

Michael J. Bugeja grew up in Lyndhurst, NJ, down the road from William Carlos Williams in Rutherford, and each summer of his youth he would vacation in Belmar or Point Pleasant. The poetry columnist for *Writer's Digest*, he has published poems in *Harper's*, *Poetry*, *The Kenyon Review*, *The Georgia Review*, *The New England Review*, and elsewhere, and his books include six poetry collections as well as *The Art & Craft of Poetry* (Writer's Digest Books) and *Poet's Guide* (Story Line Press). His latest work is *Little Dragons* (Negative Capability Press), a short story collection set in New Jersey.

Walter Choroszewksi's photographs of New Jersey have been widely published and his fine art prints are in galleries and corporate collections. He produces an annual *New Jersey Calendar*, and his books include *New Jersey: A Scenic Discovery*; *New Jersey: A Photographic Journey*; *New Jersey: Naturescapes & Details*; and *The Garden State in Bloom*, all published by his Aesthetic Press in Somerville, NJ.

John Ciardi wrote more than forty volumes of literary criticism and poetry for children and adults before his death in 1986. He taught at both Harvard (1946-53) and Rutgers (1953-61) universities, and was director of the Bread Loaf Writers' Conference from 1955 to 1972. He is perhaps best known for *How Does a Poem Mean* (1959), which became a standard text for high school and college poetry courses.

Don Colburn is a reporter with *The Washington Post* who received his M.F.A. from Warren Wilson College in North Carolina. His work has appeared in *The Nation*, *Ploughshares*, *The Iowa Review*, and *The Virginia Quarterly Review*, among others, and in 1993 he won the "Discovery" / The Nation Award.

A freelance photographer, **Donna Connor** has photographed numerous Atlantic City events, from Mike Tyson fights to Miss America pageants. Her clients include the Associated Press, Reuters, *New Jersey Monthly*, and *Atlantic City Magazine*. She lives in Sweetwater, NJ.

Bruce Curley's work has appeared in S.L.U.G.*fest*, *Mad Poet's Review*, and *Home Planet News*, among others. "The Jersey shore is a place of physical, spiritual, and creative renewal for me and has been since I was first brought there at two-weeks-old by my mother," he writes. "Wildwood was where I spent Senior Week and many other wild weeks. . . . Someone once asked me why someone would spend $5,000 on a vacation in Wildwood when they could just as easily have gone to Paris for the same money. I know the answer to that question right away: Wildwood and the Jersey shore are just more fun. That, and the food is better."

Nicholas Delo is a native of Forked River, NJ, where his father and grandfather once owned and ran a bait and tackle shop on Route 9. He has studied creative writing as an undergraduate student at Rutgers University, and the poems in this anthology were among a selection that won the university's Evelyn Hamilton Award in Creative Writing.

Emanuel di Pasquale lives in Long Branch, NJ. He is the author of a book, *Genesis* (BOA Editions, 1989), and his poems have appeared in a number of publications, including *The American Poetry Review*, *The Sewanee Review*, *The New York Quarterly*, *The Nation*, and *The Christian Science Monitor*, as well as in several anthologies.

Stephen Dunn's books include *New and Selected Poems* (1994), *Walking Light: Essays and Memoirs* (1993), and *Landscape at the End of the Century* (1991), all published by W. W. Norton and Company. Among his awards are the Levinson Prize from *Poetry* magazine, the Theodore Roethke Prize from *Poetry Northwest*, and fellowships from the National Endowment for the Arts and the Guggenheim Foundation. He teaches at Richard Stockton College in New Jersey.

Martin Jude Farawell has published his work in *The Southern Review*, *Bitterroot*, *Amelia*, *Paintbrush*, and *Hiram Poetry Review*, among others, and his plays have been produced by Off-Broadway, regional, college, and community theaters. Though now living in Pennsylvania, he grew up in New Jersey and, until his twenties, spent every summer on the Jersey shore.

Frank Finale is the former editor of the literary journal *Without Halos* and is currently poetry editor of *the new renaissance*. His poems and essays have appeared in many journals and anthologies, including *The Georgia Review*, *The New York Quarterly*, *The Christian Science Monitor*, *Negative Capability*, and the *Anthology of Magazine Verse & Yearbook of American Poetry* (Monitor Book Company). A teacher in the Toms River Regional School System, he has taught poetry workshops for the Ocean County Council of the International Reading Association, and in 1993 he received an award for his work in the promotion of literacy.

Ray Fisk founded Down The Shore Publishing in 1984 while working as a photojournalist for *The New York Times*, United Press International, and *The Philadelphia Inquirer*. Throughout the 1980s he covered Atlantic City, the Jersey shore, and southern New Jersey for numerous publications, with a 1986 stint in Haiti. In 1977 he helped establish *The SandPaper* on Long Beach Island, and worked there until 1983 as associate editor and photography editor.

Alice Friman's work has appeared in *Poetry*, *Poetry Northwest*, *Shenandoah*, and *Southern Poetry Review*, as well as publications in England, Ireland, and Australia. The author of five books of poetry, she has won the Lucille Medwick Memorial Award from the Poetry Society of America. She wrote "Blues" after she and her husband spent a weekend on the Jersey shore in the Point Pleasant area.

Maria Mazziotti Gillan is the editor of *Footwork: The Paterson Literary Review* and the director of The Poetry Center at Passaic County Community College. She is the author of five books of poems — most recently *Where I Come From: Poems Selected and New* (Guernica Editions, Toronto, Canada) — and the coeditor, with her daughter Jennifer, of *Unsettling America: An Anthology of Contemporary Multicultural Poetry* (Viking Penguin, 1994). Her awards include two fellowships from the New Jersey State Council on the Arts and an American Literary Translators Association Award for the translation into Italian of her book *Winter Light*.

John Grey is an Australian-born poet, playwright, and short story writer. His latest book is *Dance to the Window* (hozomeen press). He says he has "an ongoing love affair with amusement parks, piers, etc., and their ghosts."

Thérèse Halscheid has taught creative writing at the Ocean City Arts Center and for the Cape May Court House Technical School District and the Atlantic County Community College Continuing Studies Program. Her poetry has appeared in *Yankee*, *Footwork: The Paterson Literary Review*, *Coastal Forest Review*, and *Without Halos*, among others. Her first collection of poetry is titled *Powertalk*.

Penny Harter grew up in central New Jersey, where she lived for many years. Her involvement with the Jersey shore began in infancy, when she visited a family-owned cottage in Barnegat Light, and her first book of poems was titled *House by the Sea*. Her other books include *White Flowers in the Snow*; *Lovepoems*; *Hiking the Crevasse*; and *Stages and Views*, poems written for the woodblock prints of Hiroshige and Hokusai. She now visits the shore from Santa Fe, NM.

William J. Higginson grew up in New York and New Jersey, swimming in the Hudson River at Closter Dock, various freshwater lakes, and places along the Jersey shore — especially Cape May — since childhood. His books include

Paterson Pieces: Poems 1969-1979; Death Is & Approaches to the Edge; and *The Healing and Other Poems*, all published in New Jersey. He now lives in Santa Fe, NM, where he finds plenty of sand and sun, and misses the shore.

Jean Hollander is a lecturer at Princeton University and director of the annual writers conference at Trenton State College. She has published more than one hundred poems in such magazines and journals as *The Sewanee Review, The Quarterly Review of Literature, The American Scholar,* and *Poet Lore.* Her book of poems, *Crushed into Honey,* won the Eileen W. Barnes Award in 1986 and was published by Saturday Press. The recipient of three poetry fellowships from the New Jersey State Council on the Arts, she has also served as a panelist with the council.

A native of Atlantic City, **Barbara Helfgott Hyett** is director of the Workshop for Publishing Poets in Brookline, MA, and cofounder of the Writer's Room of Boston, Inc. She has published three collections of poetry: *In Evidence: Poems of the Liberation of Nazi Concentration Camps* (University of Pittsburgh Press, 1986); *Natural Law* (Northland Press of Winona, 1989), which includes poems about the history of Atlantic City; and the Pulitzer Prize-nominated *The Double Reckoning of Christopher Columbus* (University of Illinois Press, 1992). *The Tracks We Leave,* a new book about endangered wildlife of North America, will be published by the University of Illinois Press in 1996.

David Keller, a native of the Midwest, says he "grew up far away from any body of water, so the sea is both mysterious and soothing." A member of the U.S. 1 Poets Cooperative in Princeton, NJ, he has received several grants from the New Jersey State Council on the Arts and has published his poems in many national journals and in two books, *A New Room* (Quarterly Review of Literature Series, 1987) and *Land That Wasn't Ours* (Carnegie-Mellon, 1989). He serves on the faculty of the annual Frost Place Festival of Poetry held in New Hampshire, and on the Board of Governors of the Poetry Society of America.

Maxine Kumin, a native of Philadelphia, won the Pulitzer Prize in 1973 and was consultant in poetry to the Library of Congress in 1981-82. She has written ten books of poetry, as well as four novels and several collections of essays and short stories. She lives on a farm in New Hampshire, an environment that informs much of her writing.

Kyle Laws grew up in a small town on the Delaware Bay in southern New Jersey, and from there she migrated to Pueblo, CO. The harshness of the elements in the areas where she has lived are recurring themes that shape her poetry. Her first chapbook, *Apricot Wounds Straddling the Sky,* was published in 1986 by Suburban Wilderness Press. A collection of poems, "Yellow Woman," was published in the magazine *Look Quick* in 1988. She divides most of her time among Colorado, New Jersey, and New Mexico.

Bud Lee first went to Atlantic City as a child and visited there periodically for years afterward. He has been a contributing photographer to *Esquire*, *Rolling Stone*, *Town and Country*, *Fortune*, *Money*, and other magazines. His latest venture is serving as founder and director of the American Museum of Serious, Naive, and Children's Art, a museum of "outsider" (self-taught) art in Plant City, FL.

Vicki Gold Levi has had a long association with Atlantic City. Her father, Al Gold, was the city's first official photographer from 1939 to 1964. As a child she was Bess Myerson's page in the Miss America Pageant and a flower girl for an underwater wedding in the diving bell at Steel Pier. Today, she works to preserve the city's illustrious past. Her accomplishments include cofounding the Atlantic City Historical Museum on the Boardwalk's Garden Pier; coauthoring, with former *Esquire* editor Lee Eisenberg, *Atlantic City: 125 Years of Ocean Madness* (recently reissued by Ten Speed Press); producing and directing the historical video *Boardwalk Ballyhoo: The Magic of Atlantic City*; and serving as director of historical research for the multimedia presentation, *Atlantic City Experience*.

Joel Lewis writes that he is a "life-long Jerseyan, raised in Hudson County, and still there — Hoboken. Anthologist. Anthologized. Author of some chapbooks and one full-length book, *House Rent Boogie*. Spent years instigating magazines, reading series, and late-night poesy/coffee talk at famed Route 3 Tic Toc Diner. Currently a social worker and a freelance writer." He edited the anthology *Bluestones and Salt Hay: An Anthology of Contemporary New Jersey Poets* (Rutgers University Press, 1990).

Geraldine C. Little is the former vice president of the Poetry Society of America and the former president of the Haiku Society of America. Her published books include *Women: In the Mask and Beyond* (Quarterly Review of Literature Series, Princeton), *A Well-Tuned Harp* (Saturday Press), *Heloise & Abelard: A Verse Play* (University Press of America), *Hakugai: Poem from a Concentration Camp* (Curbstone Publishing Co.), and *More Light, Larger Vision* (AHA Books). She has received four fellowships from the New Jersey State Council on the Arts and is an adjunct professor at Burlington County College.

Peter Lucia is a native of Asbury Park, NJ, and has done work on his hometown's history (including a lengthy prose poem, *My Town — A Fortification in Words*, from which "Asbury Park — Into the Vision" has been taken). He has taught at Columbia University and the Berlitz School of Languages, has been a classical guitarist for nearly thirty years, has composed and performed music for short films and various recordings, and has been a computer imagist, consultant, and database designer for Jersey Films (at Sony Studios, Culver City, CA).

Sandra E. Lundy grew up in Philadelphia and spent most of her childhood and teenage summers "down the shore" in Margate and Ventnor. She now lives in Boston, where she writes poetry and essays and has a law practice concentrating on issues of domestic violence. Her poems and essays have appeared in *Poetry Motel*, *Hurricane Alice*, *Women's Review of Books*, and elsewhere.

Vincent T. Marchese is a professional photographer who operates a commercial studio in Paterson's Historic District, across from the Great Falls of the Passaic River. His work has appeared in many publications, including *House and Garden*, *The New York Times*, *New Jersey Monthly*, and *Victorian Homes*. He is a past president of the Advertising Photographers of New Jersey and, since 1983, the director of the photography exhibition held annually at Ringwood Manor State Park. One of his favorite places to photograph is Cape May, and his work has been featured in the Washington Street Gallery there.

H. A. Maxson was born and raised in Navesink, NJ. He has published three collections of poems, most recently *The Curley Poems* (Frank Cat Press, 1994), and his work has appeared in *The Nation*, *Commonweal*, *Poetry Northwest*, *Southern Poetry Review*, *Cimarron Review*, and dozens of other publications. He teaches English in the College Transfer Department at Nash Community College, Rocky Mount, NC.

Peter E. Murphy has published his poems and essays in many journals, including *The American Book Review*, *The Beloit Poetry Journal*, *Commonweal*, and *The Little Magazine*. He has won four fellowships in poetry from the New Jersey State Council on the Arts, as well as awards and fellowships from the Folger Shakespeare Library, the National Endowment for the Humanities, and the Corporation of Yaddo. He has also been a poetry consultant to the Geraldine R. Dodge Foundation and an education advisor to two Bill Moyers/PBS television series, *Power of the Word* and *The Language of Life*. He lives in Ventnor, NJ.

A native of South Jersey, **Shilpi Niyogi** is a senior editor in the Research Area at Educational Testing Service in Princeton. She remembers first going to Atlantic City with her parents in 1968, on the same day they received news that her grandmother had passed away in India. She also remembers how during the early 1980s the Vegas neon began bursting among the run-down salt water taffy stands on the Boardwalk. Her experiences with the city continually serve to remind her of two simple truths: that change is the one constant in life, and that the more things change, the more they stay the same.

Mark O'Hara was raised in Stratford, NJ, with several stays at his grandfather's house in Atlantic City. He now lives in Oxford, OH. His poems have appeared in *The William and Mary Review*, *Journal of New Jersey Poets*, and *Indiana Review*, among others, and he has received fellowships from the Lilly Endowment and the Ohio Writing Project.

Alicia Ostriker's books of poetry include *The Imaginary Lover* (University of Pittsburgh Press), which won the 1986 William Carlos Williams Award from the Poetry Society of America, and *Green Age* (University of Pittsburgh Press, 1989). She is also the author of *The Nakedness of the Fathers: Biblical Visions and Revisions* (Rutgers University Press, 1994) and the editor of the Penguin edition of William Blake's complete poems. She teaches English and creative writing at Rutgers University.

Joseph Paduano is a professional photographer, instructor, and author whose work is characterized by the interplay of sunlight and shadow. His publications include a calendar, *Images of the Jersey Shore* (1983); a self-published book about the shore, *Seascapes: A Photographic Essay* (1983); and several books on the art of photography published by Amherst Media. His photographs are in the collections of the Monmouth County Park System, The Port Authority of New York/New Jersey, Price Waterhouse, the State of New Jersey, Educational Testing Service, and Johnson and Johnson.

John Pember has taught English, journalism, and creative writing on the high school and college levels, and was the founder and director of the annual East Brunswick (NJ) Poetry Celebration. He has also served on the advisory board of the Geraldine R. Dodge Foundation. His work has appeared in many journals and magazines, and his chapbook, *Rope to the Barn*, was the winner of an international competition. He now lives and writes in Vermont.

Robert Pinsky, a native of Long Branch, teaches in the graduate writing program of Boston University. His books of poetry include An *Explanation of America* (Princeton University Press, 1979), *History of My Heart* (The Ecco Press, 1984), and *The Want Bone* (The Ecco Press, 1990), as well as the acclaimed translation *The Inferno of Dante* (Farrar, Straus, Giroux, 1994). "At Pleasure Bay," which appeared in *Best American Poetry* 1993, mentions sites once found around Long Branch that have since been replaced by a housing tract and a shopping center.

Tom Plante is a news assistant on the staff of *The Courier-News*, a daily newspaper in Bridgewater, NJ, and the editor and publisher of *Exit 13*, an annual publication devoted primarily to poetry with a sense of geography. A graduate of the University of California at Berkeley, he is the former editor/publisher of *Berkeley Works Magazine* and a former columnist for *The Berkeley Barb* newspaper. His books include *Wear and Tear — Selected Poems* (Crosscut Saw, 1977) and *Portable Sun* (Crosscut Saw, 1980). He lives in Fanwood, NJ, with his wife and daughter, and enjoys vacationing in Cape May Point, Ocean Grove, and other shore points.

Rochelle Ratner has published her poems in *Antaeus, The Nation*, and *Hanging Loose*, among others, and her books include *The Lion's Share* (Coffee House Press, 1992) and *Someday Songs: Poems Toward a Personal History* (BkMk

Press, 1992). A native of Margate whose father owned a business in Atlantic City, she says it has been "next to impossible" to keep her childhood experiences of beach, boardwalk, and ocean out of her poems.

Jane B. Rawlings is archivist at a nineteenth-century historical house museum in Morristown, NJ, and was a contributor to *Past and Present: Lives of New Jersey Women*. She is a graduate of Smith College and speaks five languages besides poetry. She has read at Newark Public Library and her poems have appeared in *The New York Times*, *Prairie Schooner*, *Ikebana International*, *U.S. 1 Worksheets*, and *Journal of New Jersey Poets*.

Thomas Reiter's sixth collection of poems, *Crossovers*, was published in 1995 by Eastern Washington University Press in Cheney, WA. He is the Wayne D. McMurray Professor of Humanities at Monmouth College and has received several fellowships from the New Jersey State Council on the Arts.

Susanna Lippoczy Rich is an associate professor of English at Kean College of New Jersey and the author of *The Flexible Writer* (Allyn & Bacon, 1992, 1995). She has published her work in *The New York Times*, *South Coast Poetry Journal*, *Ailanthus*, and the anthology *If I Had a Hammer* (Papier-Mache Press, 1990). She has also served as a contest judge for Saturday Press.

Michael D. Riley's work has appeared in *Poetry*, *Cumberland Poetry Review*, *Visions — International*, *Texas Review*, *Poetry Ireland Review*, *Plains Poetry Journal*, *Birmingham Poetry Review*, and *The Cape Rock*, among others. His first full-length volume of poems, *Scrimshaw: Citizens of Bone*, was published in 1988 by The Lightning Tree Press (Santa Fe, NM). He is an associate professor of English at the Berks Campus of Pennsylvania State University.

A former New Jersey resident, **Alexis K. Rotella** has published her haiku and longer poems in numerous journals and anthologies and is the author of more than twenty books. An ordained interfaith minister, she now lives in Saratoga, CA, where she practices Ericksonian hypnotherapy and astrological counseling.

Helen Ruggieri was born in South Plainfield, NJ, and grew up around Scranton, PA — "where a vacation at the shore was a necessity." Her New Jersey, consequently, consists of a series of shore towns: Toms River, Lavallette, Ocean City, and Wildwood. Now she lives in Olean, NY, where she dreams of the ocean and "summer doesn't seem like summer." Her poems have appeared in *Green Fuse*, *Earth's Daughters*, *Slipstream*, and *Snowy Egret*, and her two-part article on the pollution generated by book production appeared in *Small Press*.

Norma Voorhees Sheard is a 1988-89 recipient of a New Jersey State Council on the Arts Poetry Fellowship. She serves on the advisory committee for the poetry reading series at Princeton Arts Council and is a member of the U.S. 1 Poets Cooperative in Princeton, NJ. Her work has appeared in *The New York Quarterly*, *Maryland Review*, *Nimrod*, *Dragonfly*, *Footwork: The Paterson Literary Review*, and *U.S. 1 Worksheets*.

Ed Smith has had his poems appear in numerous magazines, including *Abraxas*, *Beehive*, *Giants Play Well in Drizzle*, *Footwork: The Paterson Literary Review*, and *Passaic Review*, as well as in the anthologies *Bluestones & Salt Hay* (Rutgers University Press, 1990) and *The Temple of Baseball* (North Atlantic Press, 1985). His two chapbooks, *Dwasline Road* and *At the Green Pool*, were published by Gaede's Pond Press in Hoboken, NJ.

John R. Smith has published his poetry in *The New York Quarterly*, *The Literary Review*, and *Berkeley Poets Cooperative*, among others. He has been a perennial poet for New Jersey Audubon since 1988.

Eileen Spinelli has published work in *A Room of One's Own*, *Muse*, and *Footwork: The Paterson Literary Review*, among others. She has also written several children's books, including *Thanksgiving at the Tappletons*; *Somebody Loves You, Mr. Hatch*; *Boy Can He Dance*; and *If You Want to Find Golden*. She lives in Phoenixville, PA.

Gerald Stern retired last year from the faculty of the Writers' Workshop at the University of Iowa. He has won many awards and fellowships and has published several books of poems, most recently *Odd Mercy* (W. W. Norton and Company). From 1956 to 1963 he taught at universities in Pennsylvania, and from 1968 to 1982 he was a professor at Somerset County College in New Jersey. "My connection with the Jersey shore is deep," he writes. "I have spent time there since I was a boy. I have traveled up and down the coast, and have considered it from the viewpoint of Philadelphia and the Pine Barrens. It is one of the great wildernesses of my heart."

Virginia Masland Stetser has had poems published in many magazines, including *The Antioch Review*, *Kaleidoscope*, *Ladies Home Journal*, *The Lyric*, and *Four Quarters*, and she is the author of four books. Many of her poems deal with life on and around the beaches of Ocean City, NJ, where she lives in a small cottage whose windows face the ocean.

George Tice was born in 1938 in New Jersey, where he still lives. He is one of America's best-known fine-art photographers and has authored more than eleven books. His works are in many museums, including the Museum of Modern Art, the Art Institute of Chicago, and the Metropolitan Museum, where he had a one-man exhibit in 1972.

Madeline Tiger teaches in the Writers in the Schools Program of the New Jersey State Council on the Arts and the Geraldine R. Dodge Foundation Poetry Programs. Born in New York City, she has been a resident of

Montclair, NJ, since 1963. She has published six collections of poetry, including *Water Has No Color* (New Spirit Press, 1992) and *Mary of Migdal* (Still Waters Press, 1991), and her work has appeared in numerous magazines and anthologies. Her awards include three fellowships from the New Jersey State Council on the Arts.

Rod Tulloss is a founder of both the Berkeley Poets Co-op and the U.S. 1 Poets Cooperative in Princeton, NJ. A past winner of fellowships from the New Jersey State Council on the Arts, he has published his poems in various literary magazines and is the author of *December 1975* and *The Machine Shuts Down*.

Shirley Warren's work has appeared in many literary journals, including *The Georgia Review*, *The Cream City Review*, and *The Lowell Pearl*. She is the founding editor of Still Waters Press in Galloway Township, NJ, and a poet-in-residence for the New Jersey State Council on the Arts' Writers in the Schools Program. Her two chapbooks, *Oyster Creek Icebreak* and *Somewhere Between*, were both published by Still Waters Press.

Warren Woessner grew up in Woodstown, NJ, and often went "down the shore" to Wildwood and Sea Isle City. He is the senior editor of *Abraxas* and has published his poems in *Poetry Northwest*, *Prairie Schooner*, and *Pig Iron*, among others. He recently published chapbooks with BkMk Press and Poetry Harbor Press.

Rich Youmans is the coauthor of *Down the Jersey Shore* (Rutgers University Press, 1993, 1994) and the former editor of a magazine that specialized in the history and heritage of the New Jersey shoreline. His articles and poems have appeared in various magazines and anthologies, including such regional publications as *Atlantic City Magazine*, *Journal of New Jersey Poets*, and *Footwork: The Paterson Literary Review*. A native of Philadelphia, he first came to the shore as a child, when his family would spend at least one week each year in Ocean City.

Karen Zaborowksi was the recipient of a 1993-94 New Jersey State Council on the Arts Fellowship in Poetry. Her poems have appeared in *Journal of New Jersey Poets*, *California Quarterly*, and *Without Halos*, among others. She teaches English at Atlantic City High School.

Acknowledgments

Grateful acknowledgment is made for permission to use works by the authors listed below. The editors would also like to give special thanks to Donna Gelagotis of Delaware Valley Poets, Inc., and to Norma Voorhees Sheard of the U.S. 1 Poets Cooperative.

A. R. Ammons: "Ocean City" and "Corsons Inlet" reprinted from *Collected Poems 1951-1971* by A. R. Ammons, with the permission of the author and W. W. Norton & Company, Inc. Copyright © 1972 by A. R. Ammons. "Somers Point" from *Poems for a Small Planet*, eds. Robert Pack and Jay Parini (Middlebury College Press, 1993). Reprinted by permission of the author.

David Earle Anderson: "With the Nuns at Cape May Point" previously appeared in *The Christian Century* and in the 1981 edition of the *Anthology of Magazine Verse and Yearbook of American Poety* (Monitor Book Company). Reprinted by permission of the author.

Scott Edward Anderson: "Gleanings" copyright © 1994 by Scott Edward Anderson. Used by permission of the author.

Walter Bargen: "Walkabout/Ocean City" from *Yet Other Waters* by Walter Bargen (Timberline Press, 1990). Reprinted by permission of the author.

Judi K. Beach: "Sunday Drive to Sandy Hook" used by permission of the author.

Jeanne Marie Beaumont: "Barnegat Light" and "Five O'Clock Terns: Loveladies, LBI" used by permission of the author.

Claire C. Beskind: "Landfill, Long Beach Island" previously appeared in A *Hard Turn: An Anthology of Poetry* (Delaware Valley Poets, Inc., 1987). Reprinted by permission of the author.

Mary C. Bilderback: "4th Street Pond at Dawn, Barnegat Light Inlet" previously appeared in *The Sandpaper*. Reprinted by permission of the author.

Laura Boss: "Last Chance: Atlantic City 3:45 A.M." from *On the Edge of the Hudson* (Cross-Cultural Communications, 1986). Reprinted by permission of the author.

Michael J. Bugeja: "Machismo" used by permission of the author.

John Ciardi: "Two Egrets" reprinted by permission of the University of Arkansas Press from *Selected Poems* by John Ciardi, copyright © 1984.

Don Colburn: "Fall Migration at Brigantine" previously appeared in *The Iowa Review*. Reprinted by permission of the author.

Bruce Curley: "On What the Future of Civilization Depends" used by permission of the author.

Nicholas Delo: "Lucky's Soliloquy on the Death of the Eel Potter" and "3 a.m., Barnegat Bay" used by permission of the author.

Emanuel di Pasquale: "Twilight: Long Branch in Early October" used by permission of the author.

Stephen Dunn: "Walking the Marshland" reprinted from *Between Angels* by Stephen Dunn, with the permission of the author and W. W. Norton & Company, Inc. Copyright © 1989 by Stephen Dunn. "Cocktail Waitress: Atlantic City" from *Local Time* by Stephen Dunn. Copyright © 1986 by Stephen Dunn. By permission of William Morrow & Company, Inc. "Atlantic City" from *Not Dancing* (Carnegie-Mellon, 1984). Reprinted by permission of the author. "Beached Whales off Margate" from A *Circus of Needs* (Carnegie-Mellon, 1978). Reprinted by permission of the author.

Martin Jude Farawell: "Ocean Gate" originally appeared in *Pudding Review* #24. Reprinted by permission of the author. Excerpt from "On the Boardwalk in Seaside Heights" used by permission of the author.

Frank Finale: "Seascape: Manasquan, NJ" previously appeared in *Poem*. "City Girls at Seaside Heights" previously appeared in *Journal of New Jersey Poets*. "Horseshoe Crabs" and "The Fishermen: Island Beach State Park" previously appeared in *Coast*. Reprinted by permission of the author. "On the Boardwalk at Point Pleasant Beach," "Twilight Lake," "River Watch," and "Island Beach State Park" used by permission of the author.

Ray Fisk: "Surfman No. 7" used by permission of the author.

Alice Friman: "Blues" used by permission of the author.

Maria Mazziotti Gillan: "First Trip to the Jersey Shore: Long Branch, NJ," "On Hearing That the Asbury Park Carousel Has Been Sold to Private Collectors," and "Weekend at Spring Lake" used by permission of the author.

John Grey: "Steel Pier, Atlantic City" used by permission of the author.

Thérése Halscheid: "Disruption" used by permission of the author.

Penny Harter: "For a Bottlenosed Dolphin off the New Jersey Coast" used by permission of the author.

William J. Higginson: "The Sea Beyond the Breakers" was commissioned for The Worlds of Stephen Crane, a conference sponsored by the English Department of Kean College of New Jersey, the New Jersey College English Association, and the New Jersey Historical Commission, and was read at

John R. Smith: "Lavallette" used by permission of the author.

Eileen Spinelli: "The Drowning" previously appeared in *Voices International*. Reprinted by permission of the author.

Gerald Stern: "The Goons Are Leaving" and "Bird Cursing" from *Rejoicings: Poems 1966-1972* by Gerald Stern (issued in 1984 by Metro Books). "On the Island" from *Lucky Life* by Gerald Stern (Houghton-Mifflin Co., 1977). "Here I Am Walking" from *The Red Coal* by Gerald Stern (Houghton-Mifflin Co., 1981). "It Was a Rising" from *Lovesick* by Gerald Stern (HarperCollins Publishers, 1987). Reprinted by permission of the author.

Virginia Masland Stetser: "Autumnal Holiday" used by permission of the author.

Madeline Tiger: "The Gull" from *Water Has No Color* by Madeline Tiger (New Spirit Press, 1992); previously appeared in *Bluestones and Salt Hay: An Anthology of Contemporary New Jersey Poets*, ed. Joel Lewis (Rutgers University Press, 1990). "Point Pleasant Beach" previously appeared in *The Asbury Park Press*. Reprinted by permission of the author.

Rod Tulloss: "Cape May" used by permission of the author.

Shirley Warren: "Learning to Float," "Half-bank, Absecon Creek," and "His Daughter" from *Somewhere Between* by Shirley Warren (Still Waters Press, 1991). "Running Aground" previously appeared in *Passager*. "Nothing Truly Terrible Ever Happened to Me" previously appeared in *Warren Wilson Review* and *Passager*. "The Bottom Feeders" previously appeared in *Coastal Forest Review*. Reprinted by permission of the author.

Warren Woessner: "Savings" and "Cape May Point" from *Storm Lines* (New Rivers Press, 1987). Reprinted by permission of the author.

Rich Youmans: "Fort Hancock, Sandy Hook," "Ocean Grove," and "Skiff Builder, 1994" used by permission of the author.

Karen Zaborowski: "Watching Them Ride the Rides" previously appeared in *U.S. 1 Worksheets*. "One Good Thing About 24-Hour Gambling" previously appeared in *Coastal Forest Review*. Reprinted by permission of the author.

We would also like to thank **Walter Choroszewski, Donna Connor, Ray Fisk, Bud Lee, Vicki Gold Levi, Vincent Marchese, Joseph Paduano,** and **George Tice** for permission to use the photographs that appear in this book.

Finally, we would like to thank **Down The Shore Publishing** for helping to make this book a reality.